Love Song of a Flower Child

*A Story of
Redemption
in the
Drop-Out Days;
the Tune-In,
Turn-On Times
of Berkeley
and Big Sur*

MARY STEWART ANTHONY

WESTBOW
PRESS
A DIVISION OF THOMAS NELSON

WestBow Press books may be ordered through booksellers or by contacting:

WestBow Press
A Division of Thomas Nelson
1663 Liberty Drive
Bloomington, IN 47403
www.westbowpress.com
1-(866) 928-1240

Cover design and artwork by Arlene Carvey-Kacik
Arlene@under thewillowdesigns.com

ISBN: 978-1-4497-6521-7 (e)
ISBN: 978-1-4497-6522-4 (sc)
ISBN: 978-1-4497-6523-1 (hc)

Library of Congress Control Number: 2012915753

Printed in the United States of America

WestBow Press rev. date: 10/19/2012

To John Francis Anthony, my husband, lover, friend,
And the chosen father of my children;
To our daughters: Aimée Denise Groen, my firstborn,
Who walked in white beside me in those years of madness,
To Lucia Claire Hiatt, a gift of grace from God,
Born in the land of my Second Birth,
To their wonderful husbands:
Thomas Rein Groen and Timothy Paul Hiatt,
Our dearest sons-in-law,
And to their children, our seven wunderkind:
Rebekah, Timmy, Jessica, and Viktoria Groen,
And Liam, Evan and Kian Hiatt;
To my family and friends scattered far and near,
To all those whose hearts are forever entwined with mine,
(You know who you are).

Author's Commentary

I actually began writing my story in 2006, while we were still living in Xi'an, China. My husband John was building playgrounds for orphanages and helping in other construction projects. I was teaching English in a high school some 40–50 hours a week. We both loved every minute of our time there, and would have stayed except we heard the Lord's call to return home in 2007 and devote ourselves to being grandparents. For more than ten years we had been only visitors to our family circle.

However, something inexplicable and very strange had happened the previous year, during our 25th wedding anniversary trip to Ireland that changed the focus of my life completely. One evening while staying at a youth hostel, I suddenly fell down, hitting a doorknob with such force that I almost lost an eye. One moment I was walking to the bathroom, and the next I was on the floor, screaming for help. Upon returning to Costa Rica where we were still serving, tests revealed that I had suffered an epileptic incident due to a large brain tumor that had been slowly growing, undetected, for years. Yet it also revealed God's mercy to me in such a powerful way. I could have fallen anytime, anywhere, and been killed. He had once again spared my life so dramatically. Thankfully, the tumor was operable and non-malignant, so we continued with our plans to go to Springfield, Missouri, for a pre-field orientation (*we were changing fields from Latin America to China*) and have the operation at a local hospital.

The surgeon had warned me that I might not be able to walk afterward, but the desire to reach China, coupled with the manifold prayers of fellow missionaries, created an opportunity for God to bestow a miracle of healing, and I walked only ten days after the operation! A slight paralysis on my right side made it necessary for some physical therapy, but the therapists and the surgeon had to conclude I had been blessed with a miraculous intervention. Amazingly, I arrived in China only three weeks late for my teaching appointment.

That traumatic event made me take stock of my life more than ever, and the Lord began urging me to write out my testimony, and to glorify Him while there was still breath in me. The following memoir records a spiritual journey from which my soul once shrank in shame and horror, but has now only unfolded greater depths of God's grace, by revealing the steps He patiently took in mercy to redeem me.

Mary Stewart Anthony
California, 2012

Acknowledgements

I owe a huge debt of gratitude to the following people who agreed to edit this manuscript, then just in its rough draft form: my beloved husband John, who has cheered me on even before I began this writing; my faithful friends Rita Gatti, along with her sister Alicia Lopez, Ruth Stevens, Lois DeFord, Steve and Annie Campbell, John and Kim Rowe; and Beverly Combs, my mentor in Missions; with special thanks to Arlene Carvey-Kacik for her beautiful artwork on the cover and Lyn Mellone for her excellent work in preparing the final revision. They came to my aid as true friends do, smilingly, patiently, lending huge doses of encouragement along with editing suggestions, corrections, additions, and subtractions. I am very grateful for their time and help in bringing this book to completion. They continue to be part of my life and are a large part of this continuing story.

Any errors that still remain, regarding names and dates of people, places, and events, are my responsibility alone, for which I ask the reader's pardon. I wrote from a very limited point of view and thus could never really do justice to the amazing depth of all the lives revealed in the story as it unfolds. The passage of time, in this case almost forty years, has both healed and eroded the process of accessing the increasingly fragile portals of memory. I have tried to be both faithful and truthful, purposefully omitting details that could be injurious to others in the telling. Kindness has been the law of my pen.

Most importantly, this was written for the glory of God, my Father.

Foreword

When Jesus comes to us, he doesn't wipe out our past. He transforms all that has been—the good, the bad, and the ugly—into a wonderful new wholeness, weaving scars into delicate lines of beauty, to be seen as if they were always meant to be. That is the music in the *Love Song* of this flower child.

To know Mary Stewart Anthony is to know a free spirit if ever there was one. A spirit, not bound as she was before she came to know the Truth, and not rebound into some Christian stereotype, but truly free. Free to dance and sing and smile. And float. I've only encountered Mary in her golden years. This is one flower child that still floats through life, seemingly unencumbered by earthbound rocky and dusty roads. Yet she is firmly grounded in what matters most.

As with the movie *Forest Gump*, this *Love Song* plays out the story of a whole generation lived through one person. Mary grew up in the midst of brokenness and a fragmented family, both fighting and fleeing the evil in her life the best way she knew how. But her fight only drove her deeper into loneliness and despair. I won't spoil the plot. I will only say that the story does not end with Mary becoming some human ideal of a saint, for sainthood is conferred from above and not below. And the saint we find here is one who is sainted through her past, not in spite of it.

The role in which I knew Mary best was when she was teaching my children in an international school in China, known then as a meticulous grammarian, a wonderful word weaver, and a woman delighting in all life has to offer. She plies these trades well in this, her own story, neither hiding nor flaunting pain, only proving that "even scars [become] insignia of tenderness."

I welcome all to read *Book One: Journey into Light,* and anticipate with me *Book Two* when this flower child meets her Marine.

Dr. Howard Kenyon
Author of *Night Shift: Crossing the Cultural Line for the Kingdom*
Oregon

Preface

"The South Coast is a wild coast and lonely"

I believe I first met Mary Stewart at a wild party on the South Coast—Point 16 to be exact. Lots of drumming, lots of drugs, Mary in typical late 60s attire: bare feet, long flowing skirt, probably a shawl over a tunic or blouse. Her daughter, Aimée, was perhaps 3 or 4 years old, wandering among the other children there. My first impressions, from afar and after meeting her husband, the tall, blond, drug-crazed drummer, Jeffrey Stewart, were these: space case, wild woman, someone hanging on to the edge with fingertips.

I lived on Partington Ridge then. She was a South Coaster and only floated in and out of my sphere from time to time. Somewhere along the way we both worked at Nepenthe. For some reason I wound up at Mary's cabin at Mill Creek shortly after her second daughter, Lucy, was born, which was several months after I gave birth to my son, Benjamin. After Mary moved to Pfeiffer Ridge, she became a regular presence as she joined the ranks of my friends who also lived on that ridge: the Morgenraths, Ruth and Jennifer Stevens, Tenny Chonin, Sylvia and Byron Rudolph, Clovis and Bruce Harris, Celia and Ray Sanborn, and others.

Mary's charming and effervescent wit was the bridge we strolled on together, between the chasm of her brilliant, esoteric, poetic mind and the absence of some very essential survival skills. A fellow struggler on this journey—in Big Sur and beyond, we walked together through the trials and joys of becoming adult, finding resolutions to life's major and minor issues, gaining some understanding, and finding some valuable wisdom. With much help from our friends and families, we have both arrived at the autumn, or perhaps even the winter, of our lives. We can look back on almost three quarters of a century, and from that perspective, tell our stories, our lamentations, and clarify our own life experiences for ourselves, with the hope of encouraging and warning the young, our young, and those who still struggle and may pick up this book.

Having been a part of Mary's story—watching it unfold over nearly 40 years, and seeing amazing changes take place in her life; seeing her new marriage grow strong and provide security, health, adventure, and contentment; and seeing her children thrive and blossom into healthy adults who have made their own families and built productive, wholesome lives in spite of very precarious beginnings—I enthusiastically offer my recommendation.

This brutally honest account of a dramatic journey from space case, wild woman, cliff-hanger, to devoted, confident, talented, wife, mother, grandmother, and world traveler, will take you through gasps of concern to tears and laughter of relief, and on to applauding this brave woman who challenged love, risked life and limb, and grabbed her golden ring.

Rita Gatti
Evansville, Indiana

* The South Coast of Big Sur, California. From "Ballad of the South Coast" by Lillian Bos Ross, as published in *Recipes for Living in Big Sur*, compiled by the Big Sur Historical Society.

Love Song Of A Flower Child

A Story of Redemption
In the Dropout Days,
The Tune-in, Turn-on Times
Of Berkeley and Big Sur

By Mary Stewart Anthony

Book One: 1937–1976

Journey into Light

"God rewrote the text of my life when
I opened the book of my life to His eyes."

Psalm 18: 24 (The Message)

Contents

Author's Commentary   vii

Acknowledgements   ix

Foreword   xi

Preface   xiii

Love Song Of A Flower Child   xv

Part One: New York   1

Chapter 1:   *Rootless and Unbound*   5

Chapter 2:   *Rites of Passage in a World at War*   11

Chapter 3:   *Root Bound in a Melting Pot*   19

Chapter 4:   *The Last Confessional*   31

Chapter 5:   *An Entrance to Bohemia*   38

Chapter 6:   *Escaping the Colossus*   45

Part Two: Berkeley   49

Chapter 7:   *The Great Disconnect*   51

Chapter 8:   *Tuning In*   56

Chapter 9:   *Turning On*   60

Chapter 10: *Dropping Out*   63

Chapter 11: *Exit Stage Left*   68

Chapter 12: *Bleeding Out in Berkeley*   73

Chapter 13: *A Mutant Queen*   79

Chapter 14: *Motherhood in Madness*   84

Chapter 15: *Endgame*   91

Photo Memorabilia   95

Part Three: Big Sur   **103**

Chapter 16: *"Les Enfants du Paradis"*   105

Chapter 17: *In the House of No Sorrow*   111

Chapter 18: *Winds of Spiritual Change*   119

Chapter 19: *Becoming a Big Sur Mama*   124

Chapter 20: *Life Dances in Circles*   130

Chapter 21: *Haven on a Hill*   136

Chapter 22: *A Stone's Throw from Hell*   140

Chapter 23: *Knocking on Heaven's Door*   145

Chapter 24: *"Like the First Morning"*   150

Chapter 25: *"They Sang a New Song"*   154

Chapter 26: *The Jesus Revolution*   157

Chapter 27: *"When the Veil Is Taken Away"*   166

Chapter 28: *Jesus Comes to Nepenthe*   173

Chapter 29: *The Vine Grows Over the Wall*   178

Chapter 30: *Exiles in Exodus*   186

Addendum: *Testimonies from the Jesus Revolution*   193

Epilogue   211

Love Song of a Flower Child

I sing of angels that ascend the air on radiant beams
And guide us to our home among the stars,
Of demons that spin a web of dread-filled dreams
And build a labyrinth to feed the jaws of death.
I sing of Light that unlocks iron chains of fear,
And banishes unholy darkness to its doom.
I sing of Love that sent a mighty King
To humbly join Himself with humankind,
And yield his life to break the yoke of sin.
I sing of Mercy freeing souls from the Destroyer,
Redeeming them by Grace, the price of blood.

Probing deep into the heart of things is the poet's passion.
Who plumbs the depth, or measures out the air
That vibrates in each spoken word?
Who writes the music for each syllable of sound?
Language, more than old Promethean fire,
Is given as a boon to man,
Illuminating hidden chambers of the soul.

If time is a dimension that always changes
Our perception of light and space,
Then reality depends on where you stand.
One day I climbed to higher ground,
And traced my faltering steps as far
As mind could bend, and found the path
Had wound with new direction.

Wisdom sifted purpose from the shadowy confusion,
Understanding bound memories into a unity of meaning,
And Beauty polished jewels buried in the dross of ruin.
It's then you suddenly realize that you had been sustained
By LOVE against all odds:
Your runaway rebellious soul escaped
The stalking terrors of the night;

Your darkened mind, once captive, broken, raped,
Had been redressed by words of truth and light.

Though we unwind genetic volumes and their mystery,
Or scale the spiral ladder to decode each sequence,
Can we divine an incorruptible inheritance?
Earthly life can be distilled to tiny drops of blood,
So that each cell may spell out health and strength
Or shadow deadly portents of disease.
None of these predicts the purpose of existence,
Or fathoms out the length of all our days.
They become another kind of sinkhole we devise.

Communion between human hearts is the truest story.
The differences and sameness fully play each other out.
Eternal verities are found somewhere in
How we touch each other, skin to skin,
This translucent veil of tissue woven
Into fabric that has bound us.
A tender heart recoils; the skin crawls.
An ice-hard heart melts; the skin burns.
This immense organ in which we hide
Has made us visible and vulnerable.
It trembles with desire, shakes with fear,
Grows fluid in beauty,
And lashes out in brute power.

We are molded underneath this fragile armor,
And strut about as bold as any god,
Defiling the earth our mother,

Profaning the heavens of our Father,
Proclaiming we are climbing ever higher
In a self-engendered evolution,
Though we keep on falling, blind and bestial,
Into a morass made of spiritual delusion.
These are the chains of our unknowing,
Dragging us to depths of our undoing,
No matter how high we leap or far we prance away.

The remains of mine, or any life, cannot be reduced
To fragments labeled in a file to calculate its worth.
Desperate to understand the seasons
And the times of my sojourning,
I dug away the stubborn clods of earth
And discovered treasured artifacts as proof.
Even scars became insignia of tenderness.
Membranes of memory, embedded with nerves
Like delicate fingers, preserved the roots of pain,
Along with tender shoots of joy,
And culled them from their burial ground.
All has been retained; not all could be recovered.
What has been written, stroke on stroke,
In frailest flesh and bone,
Can never be unwritten.

You must love the TRUTH so much
That you bless the stinging shards of light
Piercing deeper down the layering of clay.
You patiently fit pieces each to each,
And puzzle out the bundled bits of time.
The jumble awaits you day by day
As the sun's 'unhastening' eye lay bare the bones.
Then you read some old forgotten names one night
By candlelight, and remember how you prayed.
The thrill of rediscovery awakens the heart's music again,
Until you join the backwards journey in its song.

At times, such a gentle moonlight draws you
Into paths no longer discernible,
To follow down their wild ways overgrown,
That you wander into such a beauteous blur
Of worlds gone by, of worlds to come,
Of worlds without end, Amen.

PART ONE: NEW YORK
The World at My Feet

"Where can I go from your Spirit?
Or where can I flee from your presence?
If I ascend into heaven, You are there.
If I make my bed in hell, behold,
You are there."

(Psalm 139: 7–8, NKJV)

Natural life begins with a consciousness of self.
Social life begins with a consciousness of others.
Spiritual life begins with a consciousness of God.

In the beginning, our planet, like a giant molecule of water without form, had to wait in darkness for the "ah, bright wings" of God to stir the void into palpable, breathable air. The genesis for each soul's journey is the same. So we in seed form grew, wrapped in salted waters of the womb, and cannot remember the pain of being separated into light, movement, or sound. Only a mother can tell us how we came, but she often pushes it away like the placenta, as a bloodstained fact of life. The beauty and mystery of the "someone new who has just joined us" overshadows everything else: the searing pain, the gushing water and blood, the tearing of flesh, the rhythmic birth pangs overtaking the body, shaken to its root by such primordial power.

Oh, the hush of reverence and awe that comes as the pearl-like being is caught in the trough of eager hands. This tiny luminescence is able to draw out the mother's soul in deep-welled tears and soft words of wonder. "Bone of my bone, and flesh of my flesh" has become incarnate before us. We have been realized, stretched, and multiplied. The child is still attached by invisible bonds, not knowing a knife has severed the natal cord. The display of such helplessness unscrews us from the savage core of self, and undoes us into such tenderness, that our nature is redeemed through the agony of begetting another soul.

Some of us can remember a state of animal innocence, and its exquisite sensual pleasures. We were wrapped in cloaks of pretending, in the "come and get me, come and find me" games, and swapped our favorite roles with friends, enjoying the make-believe life of romp and frolic. Content in waiting for everything to unfold before us, we interpreted our origins through bedtime stories, prayers, songs, fables, and fairy tales. There were so many new sounds to imitate, gestures to mimic, and words to weave into a common language. Then came the thrill of suddenly being understood and accepted into the fluid complexity of others, ending forever the apartheid of our childhood. At last we had gained an entrance, and were identified. Now we had a place to stand and a part to learn in the cosmic drama, though the purpose for our existence had not yet been revealed.

And so my song begins before the time of my begetting, before my cry was heard, and before two very different destinies were intertwined.

Chapter One

Rootless and Unbound

My mother said she taught me all the great Irish songs she knew. Company would arrive and, early in the evening, she'd display me against the shining whiteness of the kitchen wall. To her delight, at age three or four, I warbled out all I had learned. She had successfully transmitted her heritage to me, with all its vaunting prejudice, even to the Irish lilting of her voice. From her suffering soul to mine came an injection of the miserable injustices, the shame of serfdom that she, as an Irish Catholic, had endured in County Tyrone, Northern Ireland, land that still belonged to the second Queen Elizabeth.

The good of it all was the poetry, the myths, the songs, the dance, and the music of Uncle Eddy's fiddle and great Uncle George's Jew's harp that accompanied our singing in Aunty Bea's basement kitchen. Her husband George would signal us to watch his rigid, high-kicking step dancing, while his pockets jingled with coins and keys. It was a wonder to watch his body held so still, hands at his side, steel-rimmed eyes riveted on the dream of a united Ireland, chiseled head held high, back regal-straight, while feet and legs stomped over the lingering oppressors.

Uncle George worked for a local Irish newspaper in the 1920s as a photographer and had organized many of the early IRA fundraising dances. We were often invited to them, and at the behest of my mother, he would announce me from the stage, "My niece Patsy

Steinhauer will now sing 'Danny Boy'," underscoring the fact that I was a half-breed. My nickname came from Patricia, given in honor of St. Patrick, I was told. The truth was that my father wanted his firstborn to be a boy, so he called me "Patsy," or "Pasquale." The family name, *Steinhauer*, came from the German nation then considered to be the world's Enemy Number One. I never understood why people cried when I sang. Were they sad about the war or the loss of dear old Ireland? My dad would hug me, his eyes wet with tears.

This Irish remnant family comforted my exiled mother, Susan Theresa McBride, who left the peat bog farm where she was raised with her three sisters, Mary, Margaret, and Bella. Sadly, Mother's only brother, Charles, had died at the age of seven from scarlet fever. At age sixteen, mother and her two sisters, Mary and Bella, sailed for Canada on a steamship, while Margaret stayed behind to help the family manage the farm. Her father's sister, Aunt Maryanne, became their surrogate mother, helping them take hold of a new world. The only relic of being wrenched away from family and friends was an old metal trunk that Mother kept near her bed. She had buried all her Ireland in it. The lock was broken, so I often lifted it to smell the cedar and touch the pale peach paper lining that dripped its brown edges over letters, small packets of soil with dead shamrocks, and faded photos. There weren't many smiling faces to be found in the images because there was no decent life for the *dirt-poor* Irish then. Neighbors gave parties and pitched in pennies to raise boat fares for the lucky ones who could escape. They had no hope or future in Omagh, the only city near their farm. Nothing remained for them there but the bleakness of poverty and the blackness of prejudice.

Susan's father, John McBride, had arranged to meet a neighbor's older daughter at their home. But the shy younger daughter, Margaret Byrne, standing near the great stone fireplace while fervently fingering her rosary, praying for a suitor, caught his eye. It was St. Ann, they said, who had blessed her that day to inherit a milk cow and its calf, a pig, some sheep, a horse, a flock of chickens, and turkeys. Margaret went on to became a midwife for many and learned how to extract herbal medicines from the woods. She never shared her knowledge with anyone in the family, and those ancient secrets died with her. All anyone could remember was that she always knew where to find a remedy. And the neighbors remember her skill with the concertina that accompanied her lovely singing voice. She had a fondness for her corncob pipe and a shot of *poteen*, homebrewed whiskey made from barley or potatoes, before bedtime. On the day she died, after feeding the turkeys and hens, they said she came in whispering that she was very tired, lay down on her bed, and then went peacefully to her reward.

John and Margaret did well together, and the fame of their love and devotion was even celebrated in a local song. In time, their four daughters worked as hard as any man to make a decent home near the village of Drunquin, in the leftover rubbish land, leased to them grudgingly by the British Crown. The best lands were saved for the Protestants, they were told, and so were all the jobs. After all, they were the *bloody papists*, defiling both the language and the landscape with their superstitious nonsense about saints, fairies, and banshees. Nevertheless, John McBride donated some of his land for a national school to be built, just a few skips down from their homestead. Even there they were forbidden from speaking Gaelic; instead, memorized volumes of Shakespeare rolled off their tongues. Fifty years later my mother could still quote long passages from the dramas. She would also tell us about the *Black and Tanners* who hunted them down in fields and cottages as they tried to celebrate the forbidden Mass, and then in a whisper told us she'd heard they stuffed rosary beads down a neighbor boy's throat.

Mother was born on Easter Sunday in 1910. Six years later, the news of the Easter Uprising in Dublin, which initiated the Irish Republican Army's resistance, had reached Omagh, giving rise to a bloodstained era the Irish would later call the "Troubles." Mother was baptized from birth into this cultural and religious struggle and always had such a fight in her.

Years later, when my husband and I visited the farm, we sat in the very room where my mother and her siblings were born. We visited the small stone barn where they milked the cow and raised a calf. As we walked across the peat bogs, which were over four feet thick, they felt like a stack of mattresses bouncing under our feet. The original peat barn was still there, filled with rolls of peat and stored for a year to dry. A peat fire burns almost as efficiently as coal and emits a wonderful aroma. We also heard the cries of real cuckoo birds in their fields and were told that the ancient outhouse was a later addition to the farmhouse because the bog-Irish had felt it was more sanitary to use the fields as their toilet.

My father was born out of time it seemed, to working-class Germans who had emigrated from Bavaria. He hid in my mother's shadow and would break out only after drinking his fill of beer. Reading many books made him a deep thinker, one who sorrowed over his albatross destiny as an uneducated German-American living between two world wars. Perhaps the stigma of his family name had shamed him into a half-life existence. But when Charles Henry met Susan Theresa, he saw smiling Irish eyes that sparkled like deeply set sapphires over her high rose-petal cheekbones. He let the fight within her become his, because he had no place to stand in the world then. When he listened to the lilting music of her words, he knew she would become the mother of his children.

How different this woman was, who didn't drink or smoke, from his own mother Marie, who had caused him another kind of shame. She loved to hostess penny poker games in her home and visit beer gardens. Grandpa Henry endured her drinking bouts and party ways and often had to search the streets for his wayward wife. I can still remember her lifting her newly coiffed head in such loud laughter that it would shake the rows of large amber beads that hung over her enormous bosom. She loved to sneak me a glass of beer, which she coyly insisted was just "liquid bread," because I needed fattening up.

Grandpa, the family chef, would treat us all (*and soon we would be nine souls*) to a feast every Christmas or Thanksgiving. After the meal I would climb onto their lofty bed, so full that it hurt to move, and go to sleep, wishing that delicious torment would never end. Grandma would remind us about how much Hitler had done for the country before he turned into the monster we all saw on the movie newsreels. They would let me turn the handle on the mahogany victrola to play some Caruso or John McCormick records. What intrigued me just as much as the singing was the engraved image of a dog on the front that cocked his head, listening to his master's voice coming from the machine. I don't remember a real dog ever being in our family picture. I guess animals never seemed to fit our urban lifestyle, except for the occasional cat we kept to chase away rats from our basement apartments.

The family business then in New York was Grandpa Henry's butcher shop, and he wanted his oldest son to learn the trade. Mother laughingly explained why he could never do it: her husband Charlie fainted at the sight of blood! So, as a young man he became a fisherman, enjoying a reverie lifestyle onboard a boat. He volunteered to serve in the Navy to prove his loyalty to America, and was sent to the Pacific front during the war with Japan. He spent his later years traveling as a Merchant Marine. My father tried to help his younger, emotionally retarded, brother John to overcome the stress of normal workaday demands. Despite repeated offers of help and refuge, Johnny became a drunkard and died alone in some unknown place, a runaway all his life.

The one daughter, Katherine, a slightly plump and effervescent blonde, became my favorite aunt and friend when she finally broke through my emotional shield. I don't know if it was her warm affectionate nature or her joyful spirit that coaxed my timid, preteen heart out of hiding. She managed to include me in the events of her teenage years, and took me to Frank Sinatra's first appearance at Radio City Music Hall. I remember being shocked at the audience of hysterically screaming girls, dressed in bobby sox and loafers, who imagined he was singing to them. I wondered then if being a teenager meant that I would erupt into craziness over the opposite sex. After she was married, she and her husband adopted me in a sense, before they finally had their own daughter. Every now and again they rescued me from the hand-to-mouth lifestyle of my family, providing a respite from the unspoken sadness of drudgery.

But when Susan was introduced to Charlie, she reveled in his tanned muscular body, topped with a shock of white-blonde hair. How different he was from the whistling Irish boys who had teased her while she baled hay with her father! This man had a serious quiet air about him. It would take a few beers to make him smile or even dance with her. Charlie would take her to the seaside and show off his swimming prowess. She didn't go out with him fishing, because the lurching sea reminded her of the long, sickening voyage from Belfast to Canada. Susan never suspected that the sea's pungent smell delighted him, nor that its siren voice would call Charlie away to explore the world. The sea eventually became his phantom mistress during the turbulent years of siring eight children, and caused Susan to endure many years of separation. But there was another kind of separateness to him. He was a Lutheran, while she was a Catholic. Even though it had divided his own family against him, he married her in a Catholic rectory, promising to raise their children in the Catholic faith. Her parents would have been saddened by her marriage to a Protestant, a radical departure from their ways. Her older sister Mary consented to be one of her attendants, while frowning her disapproval. Her younger sister, Bella, cheered her on with a smile. Young Susan had skillfully replaced the hymns of a church wedding with the music of her beloved bagpipes that calmed her as she walked the processional, carrying a simple bouquet of calla lilies, her favorite flower.

My mother loved to tell me how she prayed for three years before I came along, and narrowly escaped death by giving me life. She was a "bleeder," and six friends had to donate pints of blood to keep her with us. The doctor told her not to have any more children, but her Catholic faith convinced her that a mother's death in childbirth had enough merit to bypass the flames of Purgatory and fly her straight to Heaven. She defied medical advice and went on to have seven more healthy children, though not without losing three others due to severe hemorrhaging. One morning when she called me into her bedroom, all I could see were blood-soaked sheets. She asked me quietly to bring her some clean towels, and I watched her wrap them between her legs and stagger into the bathroom. "Run," she said, "and ask Alice for help!" When I told our next-door neighbor what I had just seen, she called for an ambulance, and her promptness saved my mother's life. Alice commended me for my maturity, even though I was in shock, fearing the loss of my mother. As the oldest of the family, I had become her helpmate whenever my father was absent. Alice got the others ready for school and took care of our toddlers, Susan and Kathleen. I went to school late, and shed many tears as I recounted finding my mother bleeding to death. The nuns prayed for us, because I still didn't know then whether my mother would survive.

Most of my childhood before that time is a blur due to my parents' inability to set down roots. Mother seemed to move after each child was born, like an Irish gypsy ever needing more room to cradle her young, while my father became a German gypsy, always roving the high seas, looking for the next adventure.

Chapter Two

Rites of Passage
in a World at War

We had no washing machine until the seventh child, so I washed all our socks and underwear on a metal washboard. Like a sacred ceremony, we made sure that everything we hung on lines was presented brand-spanking clean, to be scrutinized and graded by ever-nosy neighbors. I also enjoyed shopping for such a large family. Mother often sent me to the butcher shop, the vegetable stalls, the drugstore, the Jewish bakery, and the live chicken market, which I dreaded. After choosing a chicken, I couldn't wait around for the kill because the smell sickened me, and the sight of a headless chicken being chased by the butcher always set off my gag reflex. The same thing always happened when Dad prepared some fried eggs, and tried to force me to eat them. The battle always ended in a draw: me, running and gagging; and he, having to eat the eggs.

But whenever mother asked me to get my dad, her wayward husband, out of the local beer garden, I really cringed. She wanted to shame him in front of his pool hall buddies, and told me exactly what to say. "Daddy, mommy needs you to come home now!" How could he refuse his waif-like daughter? I pushed open the doors and went just a few steps into the smoky stench and noise. The music and laughter stopped as his friends called, "Charlie, your kid's here again!" Dad and I held hands and walked home together; his shame and meekness made me ache for him. Meanwhile, I never called my mother "Mommy." Her strength frightened me.

As an eight year-old coming home from school one day, I came upon a shocking sight. Luckily, I was walking alone. All our furniture and belongings had been placed on the sidewalk, in front of our rat-infested basement apartment, because the rent hadn't been paid for two months. Our shame was whispered among the neighbors and displayed on the front page of a newspaper: a picture of Mother pregnant with baby Kathleen, and her six other children draped pitifully around her. The headlines in the New York Daily Mirror went something like this: "Navy Veteran's Family of Seven Evicted, stranded on sidewalk!" (My uncle George had a part to play in that drama because my mother had called him). Well, it worked. We were taken immediately to a temporary Veteran's housing project in the Bronx, and the nine of us squeezed into a Quonset hut built for four. Despite the size, however, this was a breath of fresh air, away from city squalor to an almost suburban-like cleanliness, with open spaces and trees. The large vacant lots that surrounded us seemed to be country fields. We were close enough to my grandparent's home to could travel there by bus. God seemed to smile on us again.

The fresh air of the countryside was such a precious commodity to us city folk. The Herald Tribune, a local newspaper, actually did create a "Fresh Air Fund" that enabled concrete jungle kids like me to go to camp for two weeks or a month every summer. What a mercy that was! That's when I discovered another way of life that would haunt my youth: the joy of walking through rain-soaked woods singing, instead of running past smelly garbage cans in an alleyway; the adventure of sleeping in a tent on your own cot, instead of being lumped three or four together in a double bed; and then, the delight of eating three times a day, as much as you liked! There was the delicious smell and warmth of campfires in the evening, where we sat around on a circle of logs, and roasted marshmallows, or sang songs like "We are climbing Jacob's Ladder" and "Row, row, row your boat," or played games. During the day we had classes in arts and crafts, like painting with paper plates, weaving belts on a loom, or making leather pouches and lariats for keys and whistles. There were special times of early morning fishing from a rowboat, and sometimes late at night, the strangely sensual pleasure of skinny-dipping in a moonlit lake.

Usually our counselors were charmingly idealistic college students. One of these young ladies read *Le Petite Prince* to us in the original French before translating it into English. I had never heard such exquisite sounds, or such piercingly sweet expressions. Each night she turned our tent into a magical place, as we sat with upturned faces fastened on the book glowing under her flashlight. I strained to catch a word or two to take away with me, marveling at how her normal voice would change under the spell of lilting the French language. What a trumpet she had sounded to rouse our uncultured souls from the doldrums of ignorance! This story of an innocent creature—coming from another world and teaching the author about the beauty of childlike simplicity through the prince's pure devotion to his beloved rose—stirred my imagination and lifted me above the meaningless squalor of city life. Before I left, I had to tell her that someday I would study French just so I could read that book on my own. And I did. This book remains a precious childhood friend to me, one to whom I have introduced many other children.

And there were so many times, under the dark velvet sky studded with diamonds, when a greater Magnificence would speak to me. As city dwellers, nature's beauty had been denied us for most of our young years, with the exception of rare visits to Central Park. The stars played out their glory above me, as a friend and I lay on a grassy knoll, whispering our future dreams to each other. What mysterious language streamed down to us from other worlds, through such vast distances? Globes of light were dying and being born, leaving us these glowing fossil prints in the black celluloid of space, so we would not cease to wonder. I held no doubt then that God had once walked among them, listening to their music and tending them like seedlings, before He ever visited the earth. *But that's when God and I were still on speaking terms.*

Then, there was memory of the first garden I ever entered. The constant hum of pulsating life, and the aroma of newly watered earth, scented by plants, delighted and changed me for a lifetime to come. A German farming family who lived in upstate New York had offered to host me in my fifteenth year. The wife had asked me to help her pick vegetables, and smiled as I ate my first green beans and raw peas. They were such sweet surprises, because I had tasted only the salty canned variety, which had always made me gag, and forced me to hide them in a paper napkin. Her husband taught me to shoot a rifle as they hunted for rabbits, and to drive a tractor. My short time with them spawned a dream that someday I would plant my own garden and live in a country setting.

These seven summers of redemption enlarged me, and I always came home with a new resolve to better our family's lifestyle. My mother humored my vain attempts at any cultural reformation I undertook, because it never seemed to last more than a month. Yet, inwardly I separated myself more and more from the daily turmoil of dysfunctional family life: dad's binges caused violent mood swings, and mother took refuge in her religious rituals. She thought I was a sickly child and was ashamed of my twig-like appearance. I had inherited my father's smaller frame, his long limbs and Germanic features. She came from sturdy, strong-boned farm stock and sought out doctors who urged her to try different remedies on me. One horrific health cocktail I remember was raw egg and milk mixed with a shot glass of whiskey. The effect was an immediate rush of warmth and wellbeing that propelled me giddily on to eighth grade. I guess I always tried to curry my mother's favor through intellectual prowess since I couldn't measure up to her physical standard of health. This early rejection of my wraith-like appearance acted like a slow poison that distorted my self-esteem until puberty filled out my bones.

My German grandparents had chosen to settle in the Bronx because at that time it had a more rural setting. Whenever we visited Grandpa Henry's butcher shop with its sawdust-strewn floor, he asked us to plunge our hands into the ice-cold pickle barrel and choose one to eat. His face always smiled down at us from underneath his gold-rimmed glasses. After he sold his butcher shop, we visited the restaurant where he worked as a chef. Aunt Katherine worked there as a waitress, and we were treated as honored guests. We all slid into a big booth that surrounded an oval yellow Formica table, and had our fill of wonderful German delicacies like sauerbraten, potato pancakes, and apple strudel. Grandpa often boasted he had been a chef on the first steamer to cross the Panama Canal, which made him somewhat famous in our eyes. He said the family name, Steinhauer, meant "stone-hewer" and could be loosely translated as "Rockefeller." We all laughed, knowing it was just a fantasy claim to fame and fortune.

The Bronx was also where I took my first swan dive and broke my arm. A friend and I shared one of my roller skates each. Somewhere I had seen a picture of an ice skater dancing to ballet music. "Watch me do the swan!" I called, and did a version of a ballerina's extension. My arms were wings, and my right leg extended behind me as I bent closer to the ground. Since I didn't see a small hole in the concrete, down I went. There was an immediate sickening pain, and my right arm looked more like a broken sparrow's wing than a swan's. My father heard my friend screaming for help, but my mother's words pinned me further to the ground: "How the hell did you do that?" she yelled as she pushed the screen door open. Dad rushed over, said nothing, but cradled me like a baby as he assessed the damage, and gently carried me inside. Soon we were in a friend's car going to the hospital, while I sat—motionless and silent from the pain—on his lap.

My trophy from the operation was a full cast from shoulder to wrist, made rigid with an iron bar from wrist to shoulder. I learned how to write, eat, and read with my left hand. The healing process took six months. Finally the day came for the cast to be removed, and I remember standing in a large operating theater surrounded by doctors who seemed quite pleased with the results. I wanted to hide my puny arm, but they insisted I show it off as proof of their success! It was humiliating to be treated like a medical specimen, instead of being cuddled like the frightened little girl I was. My father had been my only companion through this journey, and it was the closest I had ever felt to either of my parents.

My younger brothers, Charles and Johnny, and I attended a very strict Franciscan Grammar School, where the nuns were quick to rap knuckles and slap palms with a ruler. My youngest brother Edward stayed at home along with Margaret and Susan, as we waited for baby Kathleen to be born. Just around the corner loomed my Confirmation, a big rite of passage in a Catholic girl's life. I hoped it would be as sweet as my First Communion had been three years earlier. That particular memory still radiates from the early dark corridor because it was my first God-conscious moment. There were months of catechism classes after school that guided our thoughts and expectations, and I took it all very seriously. The dress, veil, gloves, and purse, borrowed from cousins, were mended and washed. The shoes and socks were brand new. The nuns gave us each a new prayer book and rosary. I walked down the aisle in a white dreamscape lit by candlelight. Auntie Bea had wrapped my thin blonde hair in rag curls the night before, and I sported ringlets for the first time in my life. I had been prepared as a bride to meet this God who was hidden in a golden tabernacle, mounted high on a linen covered altar, gleaming with tall white candles, and crowned with flowers.

Nothing could dissipate the shine of that day, not even the gloomy rain that fell as my mother and I walked quietly home. We were silent under the black umbrella as we stepped around puddles in the potholes along the glistening sidewalks. Nothing would mar the purity of this passage. Perhaps mother was locked into the memory of her own sweet ritual in Ireland. She hurried us home and made some tea and toast, afraid I would faint from the prolonged fast. But I didn't want to disturb the God who had just become my Heavenly Bridegroom. I hid in my room wondering how long it would take for the host to melt inside me, until hunger finally drove me into the kitchen.

Home seemed such a quiet place then with only five children: Charles Henry Jr., named after his German grandfather; John Vincent, named after his Irish grandfather; Edward Joseph, named after mother's only brother; and Margaret Ann, named after mother's sister, left in Ireland. Our Margaret Ann became such a beauty that she won the New York Daily Mirror's "Charming Child Contest."

But the world was at war with a double-headed monster: Nazi Germany and Imperial Japan. Dad had volunteered to fight Hitler to prove his loyalty to America, but was commissioned instead to serve on a battleship headed for Japan. The year 1945 was punctuated by both V-E Day and V-J Day. Quiet streets that once had waited for the dreaded wail of sirens now erupted into dancing. Green-shaded windows that once had hid us from the threat of air raids were thrown open, spilling out toilet paper streamers. Children sat on friendly shoulders watching their parents and neighbors dancing, sharing beer bottles, and waving flags. America had entered the world stage singing songs of victory.

How triumphant it must have felt to those women, after years of standing in line with ration books, and working late hours in factories dedicated to the machinery of war! But could they ever return to a simple Betty Crocker lifestyle, spiced with Hollywood scandals and romances, loud baseball games and football rallies, and swing dance music bands? Women had joined the workforce, and a new brand of female emerged, a "Rosie the Riveter" flexing her muscles, one that had found worth and purpose beyond the home.

Dad had been gone for over a year, and my beautiful mother filled her lonely hours with a friend she introduced as "Uncle Joe." He took us to the zoo and bought us ice cream cones, something I didn't remember my dad ever doing. When my father returned from the Pacific, we never mentioned Uncle Joe and his treats. A child has nothing with which to judge a vague memory like this, except conflicting feelings of confusion and fear. Daddy was our only hero then. He had been wounded by shrapnel while at his gunner's post, and looked so tanned and handsome in his white sailor suit. Soon my mother burgeoned with child again. Little Susan Theresa was born in July and mother finally had her own namesake.

In later years, I never mentioned this affair to my mother, not wanting to shame her. But I often had to wage an internal battle not to wield it against the self-righteous veneer that she hid behind. The law of love would eventually overturn my guilty verdict, and release her from my judgment. How could I have known then how much I would need this same mercy for myself later on?

Just before my Confirmation I had been reading Carroll's *Alice in Wonderland* rather than the usual saint's biography. Alice's adventures were hilarious, full of surprises, confusing and spellbinding. I envied her quick-wittedness, her ability to morph and adapt to different situations. The many fairy tales I had ingested seemed anemic in content, though rapturous in moral beauty. Their plots were predictable, but their magic compelling. Each colorful illustration delighted my soul, alluring me to a dreamland of distant, unknown kingdoms. But Alice was not a princess with a destiny. She was a naive schoolgirl caught up in an impromptu whimsy. She made me laugh inside and out, and because nothing seemed impossible to her, she became my unlikely—and unsaintly—heroine.

The rite of Confirmation is a ritual remnant of the Holy Spirit's Baptism of Fire, meant to transform young Catholics into soldiers of the Lord. We were asked to kneel and endure a white-gloved slap on the cheek from the local Bishop, who would then pronounce a new name over us. Our passage into Christian maturity was sealed by this name, as evidence of our new identity in Christ, and was usually chosen from the ranks of Christian heroes. But Alice was my heroine of choice and I loved that it shocked the nuns. Of course it really horrified my mother who often lamented, "But Alice is not a saint's name! What will the Bishop think?" My defense was surely inspired. "But mother, think of how beautiful it will sound in Latin: "Mareeea . . . Patreeceea . . . Aleeceea." I sonorously intoned them in my best Church Latin. She wavered and again mumbled weakly, "But Alice is not a saint's name!" Then I closed the mouth of the lioness with a surprisingly grandiose retort, "Then I will make it one!" This was a rare one-upmanship moment for me. Usually her prickly words would make my tongue go numb.

At Confirmation then, I was no starry-eyed child bride walking down the aisle, but a supposedly victorious battle-scarred soldier. My aunt had to cut the dress sleeve to fit around the bulky cast that guarded my broken arm. I wore a red beret instead of a veil, to symbolize a soldier's bloodstained helmet. The nuns pinned a red ribbon on my dress like a badge of honor. With head bowed and hands folded, I waited to hear the lovely Latin song of my name, and steeled my cheek for the Bishop's slap. Instead I felt nothing and left the altar with a nagging emptiness. This token spiritual experience would have to suffice me for the next twenty-six years.

Chapter Three

Root Bound
in a Melting Pot

The wheels of our German-Irish gypsy wagon soon began to roll onward. Kathleen Agnes, the seventh child, was born and became the new imperative for mother to move. In fact, we even called this little one "the gypsy" because she was the only dark-haired beauty cradled among our row of towheads. Mother had endlessly questioned the nurses at the hospital to make sure she belonged to us. The head count was now up to nine in a space built for five at the most, so we were squeezed out into a brand new seven-room apartment in a Manhattan low-income project. This was the most luxurious setting we had ever known: four bedrooms, a living room, dining room, and a kitchen. All of us learned to share the one bathroom without much squabble. The smile of God had again changed the tide of our fortune. Everything was clean and orderly. We were like the fragile, newly planted trees in the concrete playgrounds, ready to put down roots. From this place of new beginnings we would each launch our individual lives. Here we exchanged our rootless wanderings for becoming root-bound in a lower east side melting pot.

To the south of us was the Bowery, a no-man's land, lined with the disenchanted down-and-outers. It was near the Brooklyn Bridge that I vowed I would never cross, and never did. Brooklyn was enemy territory for any true Yankee fan! A tree-lined parkway was the eastern boundary, edged by the East River across the street from us, where we spent many a hot summer's night sitting on benches and talking until early morning in the welcome breezes. As the trees later filled out, we could escape from the broiling sun, and rest on the park grass, cool and damp from the sprinklers. During this time of Dad's extended sobriety, he held a job as a tugboat captain, and we would stand and proudly wave at him from the railing.

To the north of us was our swimming hole, a large city pool in a cage, a high chain-linked fence that protected us from endless traffic. In the summer it jumped with screaming small fry like us who wouldn't go home until we were lobster pink from our boil in the green chlorinated water. To the west of us was the infamous Greenwich Village. My brothers went there before I did, but only to ogle and ridicule those they then called "queers" and "weirdos." I would explore the outer limits of this place but didn't make the cultural leap until a few years later, when I had enough French in my craw and enough savvy on the new existentialist philosophers like Sartre, Camus, and Simone de Beauvoir. During my college days, I went fully armed into these cafés to speak French with aplomb, enjoy a glass of wine, discuss the latest books and ideas, and learn the game of chess.

The living room of our new home was gradually fitted out with brand-new furniture, and not the leftovers of other households. To my delight Dad asked me to go with him and choose a living room set, lamps and tables, and matching drapes. He was in a very sober state of repentance, having recently been baptized a Catholic, and had even worked for a while as a handyman at our grammar school in order to help pay our tuition. The boys got the largest bedroom with two new sets of bunk beds and dressers. Margaret, Susan, and I shared a room filled with hand-me-downs, and Kathleen had the smallest room for her nursery.

After raising seven children, my mother got her first washing machine, with the brand name "Easy." Though late in coming, it definitely made our lives easier. The wringer on the top magically flattened all the clothes almost dry, and Mother taught me how to carefully do this part, without catching my fingers in the rollers. It seemed luxurious compared to using the washboard. I had been her quiet little helper since the age of five, and remember standing on a step stool to reach the ironing board, carefully guiding the very heavy iron over all the flat work she had given me. Now I was able to use this skill at the apartment building, and took in pillow bags of ironing from the neighbors as a way of earning money. She also taught me how to sew and darn socks by hand. I still enjoyed hanging out a perfect line of wash in the sunshine for her. During the winter rains and snow our apartment was filled with lines and wooden drying racks filled with wash placed near the steam radiators in every room, and Dad laughingly said it looked like we lived in a Chinese laundry.

My dad should have been the family chef, and I loved to watch him prepare food for special occasions. Unfortunately he had to perform that role when drunk. These were rare moments because he was *pater familias in absentia* most of the time. He taught me to love baseball and took me out a few times to Yankee Stadium. I remember seeing Babe Ruth hit a homerun and trot the bases in his last public appearance, and enjoyed watching other heroes of the game like Joe DiMaggio, Mickey Mantle, Whitey Ford, and Yogi Berra. It was during one of these brief outings that my heart swelled with longing for him to be my strong protector, my mediator, my interpreter and guide for the mysterious world that lay before me.

You would think that being the oldest had enough clout, but a time came when I had to fight for another kind of recognition just before entering puberty. It may have been my first confrontation with him. "Dad, I'm a woman now, and I want you to call me by my real name, Mary!" His gaze shifted from my face to my figure, and he smiled. Dad took my part and actually trained the whole family to honor my request. I was hardly ever again called that hated name "Patsy" . . . at least not to my face.

I would watch in fascination, sitting at his feet, as he blew perfectly shaped circles of smoke that smelled like exotic incense to me. He never drank his beer from a bottle or a can, always from a glass. I learned to wait until the first bottle was gone but he was still lucid before I talked with him. The newspaper was always his first because he wanted to read the sports section and do the crossword puzzle. The living room was his throne room, and the place where his beloved books were displayed. Whenever I looked at the titles and asked about reading *Grapes of Wrath* or *East of Eden*, he would say firmly, "No, not yet." And so I waited for his permission, and it came shortly after I graduated from high school. He ceremonially handed me James Joyce's *Ulysses* to read, though I wasn't mature enough to ingest the raging river of words called "stream of consciousness." What a mind-bending read! It forever changed the tenor of my literary tastes and began a quest to explore all the great Irish authors: Joyce, Synge, Hopkins, Yeats, Swift, and others. Then I expanded the horizons of imagination further through the great science-fiction writers: Heinlein, Asimov, Bradbury, and more. All these books became the well-traveled highways of endless discussions during my high school and college years.

At that time Dad went to Delahanty Institute, a school especially for the World War II veterans, and took courses at night on how to make a shortwave radio and a television. It may have been the time he finally earned his GED. Then he became the neighborhood hero when he brought home an 8-inch TV, something none of us had ever seen. It had no cabinet, so all its wires, sockets, and coils were left exposed. The screen looked like an alien's eerie green helmet, bulging out from a space machine. Our living room was soon very crowded with kids watching *Kukla, Fran and Ollie* and also *Howdy Doody*. We had been suddenly elevated to a "first on the block" status, a rarity for us.

Dad's favorite toy was the shortwave radio, because he enjoyed being connected to the world at large. Those days may have been his only moments in the sun. He lived quietly among us in smoke and shadows, a man of vagaries, beaten down by life in slow motion. His drinking caused him to float from one job to another, and our finances always fluctuated between times of sufficiency, or abject poverty augmented by welfare assistance.

Meanwhile, Mother worked tirelessly for the family like an internal combustion machine to make up the shortfall. She took a small job at the project's laundromat, and even worked nights at a hotel under her sister Mary's tutelage. Our meals came from canned goods mostly, as her wifely duties in the kitchen never gave her much pleasure, so she never passed on any cooking skills to me. Her imagination and passion were framed by politics and religion rather than by household chores, since her young soul had been torn apart by the Irish turf wars. She eventually became a card-carrying member of the John Birch Society, and an increasingly legalistic Catholic. Her hatred could now be directed at Commies and Jews. She anointed Joseph McCarthy as her point man in the war against infiltration and conspiracy. This lopsided patriotism only further alienated her from our extended family.

Yet her true genius showed in a flawless recitation of poetry and Shakespeare, which delighted all who heard her. Those were her shining moments and my sweetest memories of her in our family. She constantly wrote pithy letters to newspaper editors, unafraid to share her point of view or displeasure, and seemed to have found her public voice in those finger-pointing "pinko" days. To see her name in print delighted her, and she was eager to discuss the latest political fiascos or conspiracy theories with any who would listen. Her good works evolved from a combination of getting people registered to vote and getting them baptized into the church. At times I was her assistant, listening to her quote scripture: "Other sheep I have . . . them also I must bring." I was embarrassed by her boldness as we knocked on doors. Her questions to the local Hispanic immigrants came rapidly: "Are you married, baptized, American citizens, registered?" Her reputation as the neighborhood recruiter and proselytizer gained her some modicum of respect.

The Jacob Riis Projects where we lived slowly began to change in appearance and ethnicity, in contrast to the Peter Stuyvesant middle-class projects that we passed on the way to school and church. Our newly painted buildings were soon scarred by graffiti and grime, and had deteriorated into slum dwellings by the time I graduated from the local grammar school. The hallways began to reek of urine and abandoned garbage bags. Consistently broken elevators made life miserable for some of the elderly. Mother was positive both the Blacks and Puerto Ricans were the culprits, lamenting, "Those poor ignorant savages, God help them!" She knew she had good reason to suspect them after she was actually accosted by one in an elevator, her wedding ring yanked from her finger and her purse stolen. My parents had moved to an upstairs apartment to get away from the increasingly noisy hallway downstairs. *Many years later, when she had been pushed down on the sidewalk and robbed again at knifepoint, my father decided it was time for them to leave New York City, which they did, after living there for nearly half a century. But that's another story.*

A blond bouncy Polish girl named Mara had become my best friend in grammar school and mentored me through the early stages of adolescence. She began by asking me to try on her bra, and just smiled when I told her it fit. It took courage to ask my mother to buy me one of my own, but what really shocked her was when I told her I had bought tampons for my period. "One doesn't touch that part of your body," she said. Had her own mother ever prepared her for life? Or did the Irish Catholic culture treat human sexuality as if it were a caged animal hiding in some dirty dungeon, surrounding it with morality tales and sordid jokes? They must have felt that children had to be protected from the inevitable assault of such a monster that escaped now and then, and lured the innocent into its lair.

Mara had also introduced me to her friends who hung out in the nearby soda shop. Someone always had nickels for the jukebox; we drank egg creams and cherry cokes, and danced on the sidewalk. I remember stuffing my first bra with tissues in order to impress a certain young man who lived in our project. My first crush passed swiftly enough, and Mara was my savvy elder sister, an alter ego who kept her eye on the boys around us. She had lost her mother at age three, and was both daughter and homemaker to her father, a burly truck driver who spoke with a thick Polish accent and who drank too much. Their small apartment was right across from the school and smelled of beer and cigarettes all the time. It made our new apartment look palatial.

I was still a devout Catholic girl while attending Immaculate Conception Grammar School, going to daily Mass and communion, and making novenas. My book diet then consisted mostly of saints' biographies and a smattering of Augustinian theology. I searched relentlessly for spiritual secrets to obtain an essence they called "holiness." They seemed to possess an extrasensory perception of another world, and their lives were quietly lived somewhere between earth and heaven. When a nun invited me into the convent, I marveled at the silence, the spacious clean floors, the swish of robes, and the whisper of rosary beads. Perhaps here was a place to set my sights, to pursue the undefined hunger that assailed me. I locked that memory in my heart, and felt sure my vocation was to follow in the footsteps of Therese of Lisieux and Teresa of Avila, both cloistered Carmelites.

Even though I was cutting my spiritual teeth on some old sainted bones, my soul was bombarded with doctrinal questions. I resented the way my mother and others prayed the rosary during the time of Mass. It didn't make sense for them to be praying to Mary while Jesus was being sacrificed again on the altar. Then I began to question the primacy of the Roman Catholic Church. Once, in eighth grade, I participated in a class debate over the issue, "There is no salvation outside the Roman Catholic Church." Appointed to be the devil's advocate, I argued with my priest from what I understood Augustine's premise to be: that there was a *Church Visible,* and a *Church Invisible and Universal,* and no one could rightly say who belonged to either one. It became, in essence, the starting point of my growing dissention. For example, in class one day, each student was asked to name their saint. When it came my turn, the nun said, "Well, yours is certainly the Blessed Virgin Mary." When I objected and said, "No, sister, my namesake is St. Mary of Egypt, known as Mary Magdalene," she was embarrassed. I had done my homework on sainthood, and knew I was a sinner. This impromptu answer proved to be prophetic and revealed that my soul's compass was already pointed in the direction of exploration and rebellion.

Mother danced a jig in the kitchen and put on the teakettle when I announced that I had won a full scholarship to Cathedral High School. She did this whenever some good news came her way. Cathedral High was located in the middle of the city, and that meant I had to take the subway from the Lower East Side to Lexington Avenue and Fifty-First Street. The all-girls' school was directly across from the elegant old-world Waldorf Astoria Hotel and one block from the monolithic St. Patrick's Cathedral on Fifth Avenue, cultural icons that belonged to an upper level of society. My Aunt Mary had worked as a housekeeper for many years at the Hotel St. Pierre, and had often told us about such wonders. These were portals to another world, where people dressed nicely all the time, not just on Sundays, and where porters carried their luggage, opened their doors, and white-gloved doormen whistled for their cabs.

But this never stopped my mother from proudly marching

all her seven children down this same street, past the Cathedral, carrying Irish and American flags, and signs that said, "England, get out of Ireland!" We had observed the St. Patrick's Day Parade as solemnly and as faithfully as going to Sunday Mass. The sound of wailing bagpipes made tears well up in us all, and the sight of kilted warriors prancing to drums brought cheers of *"Erin go bragh!"* from the streets lined with Irish immigrants. That's how I learned it was good to be Irish, and how proud I was that everyone in New York City seemed to join in the celebration. I pushed my German heritage far behind me, and whenever I was asked, felt ashamed to say my last name for many years.

The weekly underground journey proved to be horrific. Early morning rush hour meant being pushed and shoved inside a slimy subway train, and goosed by the ever-present perverts. Because I carried so many books, I was exposed and helpless to their probing fingers in the crush of travelers. And I was ashamed to speak up for the first year. I hated myself for being such a coward, until I finally got the courage to yell a practiced profanity or two against the assault and the attacker. People would smile and give me a bit more space, or even offer me a seat.

School was another kind of social exposure that provided emotional and mental growth spurts. Most of my classmates were from the upper edges of the middle class. We were made equal by wearing uniforms: our plain navy blue jumpers and white blouses. Only a few friends knew that I could afford only two uniforms. And I was relieved that not everyone could afford the matching blue blazer. Each evening I washed the blouses and stockings by hand in the bathroom. If my stockings ran, I would borrow an eyebrow pencil to mark a line up the back of my bare legs to pass the nuns' inspection as we walked in the hallways during each class change.

Before graduating from grammar school, my first movie date was with Jimmy, a good Catholic boy from Stuyvesant Town. We sat almost motionless and sweaty until I let him drape his arm around my shoulder. Again, mother was thrilled I had climbed the social ladder a wee bit with an Irish lad. But my true debut into middle class society came in my high school sophomore year, when I was invited to attend a formal Sweet Sixteen birthday party. Tessa was a doctor's daughter who offered to accompany me on her accordion whenever I sang the Bach-Gounod "Ave Maria" during Christmas season. She was outgoing enough to become the class comic, regaling us with nonstop Italian humor, and remained a loyal friend throughout our school years. She sensed how nervous and unsure I was about accepting her invitation, and gently expressed concern that it might be a hardship for me. Instead, I assured her that I was honored to come and would manage. Mother and I found a knee-length gown that was strapless, with a royal blue velvet top over a full white tulle skirt, matching blue shoes and elbow length gloves. She added her own pretty white shawl, a faux-pearl necklace, clip-on earrings, and a white beaded clutch, and was ecstatic to see her daughter transformed into a *debutante* for a day. This was my first and only excursion as a young student into such an elegant atmosphere.

Our escorts from the Xavier Military Academy came dressed in full uniform to pick us up by cab and transport us home. It may have been a little awkward for me to give my appointed escort an address from our neck of the woods. Yet, I would not let anything spoil this magical evening, and it has remained picture-perfect in my memory. We enjoyed the luxury of a catered dinner at a beautiful hotel, replete with silver candelabra, linen tablecloths, floral vases, and attentive waiters. After dinner we enjoyed some ballroom dancing with our partners. Everything was a brand-new experience, especially the food choices. It was like being at a masked ball, where I could change my identity for one evening.

Acceptance on this level was a joyful step out of the cold subterranean tunnels of my childhood into a warm sunshine of smiles and laughter. I began to enjoy life, and the person I was becoming. New friends taught me to dance the Jitterbug and the Lindy Hop during recess in the classroom. Though I was never the popular one, they succeeded in drawing me out of my characteristic introspection. The more rebellious ones taught me how to sneak a smoke or two in the café directly across the street from school during my senior year. Meanwhile, life at home grew tenser as the cultural divide between my parents and me widened. After all, my new persona had a mind and voice of its own, and even manifested a bold contentiousness. Is it possible to outwit the laws of DNA, of blood and chromosomes conspiring to set us into the concrete image of our parents? I was already exhibiting my mother's religious spirit and her testy combative personality.

My first introduction to the immense Oxford English Dictionary, in the school library, transfixed me by the sheer number of words at my disposal, and I remember turning the tissue-thin pages reverently. My father's crossword mania DNA and love of books had successfully been transferred. How else could I explain this persistent lust for words, these alpha and omega bits of information that I would greedily collect? I was fascinated by the story of how the family tree of English had flowered into a universal language from such primitive Anglo-Saxon German roots by the grafting in of Greek and Latin branches. Ever since then I have pursued looking up each new word's root structure. Even the phrase "morphing into an insatiable bookworm" cannot adequately describe my state in those days; the library was where I wanted to live, to work and to dream. The sight and smell of moldy, dusty books alleviated my soul's hunger, and I consistently checked out the maximum number of books allowed every week.

Hungry to ingest whatever information was thrown my way, I was desperate to learn all I could. French, Latin, English, Physics, History, and Music were my favorite subjects. Algebra had been fun in the beginning, and I learned enough to be on the factoring team, but the agony of trying to memorize theorems in Geometry stumped me. They never made any sense, and to my chagrin, I had to be left behind as my honors class continued on in Trig and Calculus. The only way I would be allowed to graduate with them was by taking the requisite Geometry in college and having that grade transferred to my record. But the real joy of those school years was the discovery of other cultures and other worlds. Catholic girls were required to learn French and Latin, while their male counterparts studied Greek and German. For once I was glad to be a girl, and French became a deliciously difficult music in my mouth. Learning it caused me to develop a French alter ego that I fully played out during my remaining student years.

It was also during my sophomore year that Mother had an unexpected pregnancy, a surprise that sometimes visits just before the onset of menopause. It was delightful to me, but must have been so hard on her, at age forty-three. There would be a sixteen year gap between the youngest child and me, the oldest. I asked mother if I could be the godmother and name her. We agreed on the name Bernadette Rose, inspired by the movie *The Song of Bernadette*. As this delicate blond angel girl joined our family, I felt the first stirrings of a maternal instinct. I was so proud to stand up for her at the baptismal font and take on spiritual responsibility for her soul. A strong bond formed between us in those early years. How I loved wheeling her around in the stroller, secretly hoping that someone would ask if I were her mother! But my father had decided this child would really be the last one, and pleaded with his wife to have a hysterectomy, which she did soon after. Bernadette, the last flowering of my mother's womb, finally closed the childbearing chapters of her life. Against all medical odds, she had borne eight healthy children, but endured the pain and loss from three miscarriages that almost cost her life.

Then a theological bombshell exploded during my junior year. A Dominican nun, her face flushed with excitement, opened the door to our classroom and announced that Pope Pius XII, to celebrate the beginning of the Marian Year, had once again designated Mary to be the "Mediatrix of all Grace, and Co-Redemptrix of the human race"! She was breathless with joy and I was speechless with shock. This was the first time I had ever heard Mary referred to in this way. Was it our duty as Catholics to swallow this doctrinal camel whole? This teaching had originally come down *ex-cathedra* from Pius IX in 1854. Somehow my father's Lutheran DNA of *sola scriptura* switched on to override this error, and threw me into a doctrinal quagmire.

After recently winning two hundred dollars in a nationwide essay contest, I had been appointed editor of the school newspaper. That meant I had to write articles about Mary. How was it possible to put Mary on the same level as Jesus? She was a human being, chosen to bear God's Son, who was destined to pay the price for mankind's sin by His death on the cross. Jesus was our Redeemer, not Mary. Equating Mary with Jesus made me cringe, and didn't make any sense.

From then on as we walked the hallways between classes, I wore the tortured mask of piety to hide the turmoil of my soul. A very intuitive nun once remarked that I looked as though I were about ready to explode. How could I tell her the truth about my doubts and my dissension? At that point my childhood dream of becoming a Bride of Christ as a cloistered Carmelite began to fade into unreality. Somehow I knew who Jesus was, and stood loyally at his side. There would be a harsh consequence for my doctrinal dissent much later, like being branded as a heretic.

Chapter Four

The Last Confessional

Ironically, while navigating those murky waters, I trained for an audition in Otto Preminger's film, *Saint Joan*. He was conducting a nationwide talent search, and had come to New York. After careful research into Joan's trial, some expert coaching from my British girlfriend's mother, and sporting the latest *gamine* haircut from Greenwich Village, I was convinced that Joan and I were soul sisters. The taxi driver who drove me to the audition gently tried to break the spell. "Honey, I'm tellin ya, this guy's gonna choose some dumb dame from Iowa, not a cute New York chick like youse. I'm telling ya, it's a publicity stunt!" But I held fast to my dream, that is, until I walked into the auditorium filled with drama queen hopefuls.

A sickening feeling that the taxi driver had been right settled into my gut as I heard the others deliver their lines with such abandon. But surely Mr. Preminger would be able to overlook my quavering voice and trembling limbs, to see that I was God's chosen girl, the one who truly embodied Joan's spirit? I could barely utter my lines on cue before I was ushered off stage. Many people were praying for me, including my alma mater, but the taxi driver had been a prophet in disguise. Actually Preminger did choose a beautiful farm girl from Iowa, named Jean Seberg. The movie was made in France, and it didn't seem to matter if Miss Seberg had ever learned French. The publicity did help to sell the movie, which wasn't critically acclaimed, but I could never bring myself to see it. As the song goes, Jean didn't "return to the farm," after seeing the glorious city of Paris, but stayed on to act in many French movies. There is no doubt that I would have been swallowed whole by the charm of French culture, but I certainly envied her being chosen instead of me.

The fact that I tried so hard to win had elevated me to a local celebrity status, especially in the soda-shop crowd, and helped heal my sense of failure. My family was especially proud of my effort, though my brothers loved to taunt me with, "So you wanna be Joan of Arc, do ya?" They would bind my hands and feet, blindfold me, tie me to a clothesline pole, and pretend to burn me at the stake. They went as far as setting crumpled newspaper on fire at my feet, before brotherly good humor kicked in and they stomped it out. This stunt, and the times they would chase me around the house, wielding Dad's Samurai sword in the air, was all payback for my years of being mean to them when they were little. Life metes out its little justices in fair measure.

It must be said here that my spiritual life was lived in the realm of imagination only. I was a *wannabe* saint, a phantasm of painted halos and wings, inhaling clouds of incense from the altar. I imagined the ancient Sphinx to be a symbol of my immense spiritual thirst. I pitied her being planted in a desert of blind wanderings, consigned to sit and slowly disintegrate in a maelstrom of sandstorms, and unable to reach a true oasis of rest. This is when God and I had a "rumble." In all our previous encounters I had mimicked the language of great saints, even writing Him a passionate love letter, signed with my name smeared in blood, obtained by pricking my finger with a knife. I probably burned the letter out of fear of its discovery. *I wonder what words I said to Him then, this One who had tracked me now all the way to this wilderness? A disturbing image persists in memory of a moment when I was looking up at the sky where I imagined He lived. We were locked in an invisible combat when my angry soul cried out, "What do you want from me?" He seemed to answer me with the simple words, "your life." I shook my fist at Him, and shouted "No!" Then I felt the air around us suddenly whoosh into a deadly silence, shaking us apart.*

From then on I walked around in the spiritual vacuum of lostness that some might call "liberty," or the absence of fences. When I was a very young child, some close friends of my parents enabled me to make a tiny record of my favorite song then, "Don't Fence Me In," popularized by Roy Rogers. The words echoed the rebel longings of my soul. God had lovingly let me go my own way, as He always does with His prodigal children. My next step was to go to a priest and confess that I couldn't accept the church's doctrine about Mary. This happened to coincide with my graduation from high school. He sternly warned me about committing heresy, and the danger of being ex-communicated, and he forbade me to receive communion or any of the sacraments until I repented. This mini-drama took place within the veiled walls of a dark confessional between a rebellious teenager and a duty-bound priest. In anger I responded, "No one is going to tell me I can't receive communion anymore!" and walked out. That was the last time I ever entered a confessional.

I felt like an outcast, a young divorcée fleeing from the vows made to her God, and could find no place on which to set my spiritual feet. In secret defiance I still went to Mass, thinking I had to have this "Bread of Angels," and keep what I thought was a portion of God. This way, Jesus and I could still be friends, even though His Father and I weren't speaking, and I wasn't praying to His mother anymore. No one knew what had happened deep inside the core of my being, that double helix where the issues of life and death are resolved, for good or for evil.

Thankfully, my friend Mara kept me grounded by instructing me in the normal jargon of clothes, boys, and pop music. She was my connection to the 'hood and took me to lively Polish dances, and introduced me to her circle of family and friends. Those were also the days of Alan Freed's Rock and Roll, or "jungle music" as Mother called it whenever she caught us listening to his radio program. Since we no longer lived mainly in lace-curtained Irish ghettos, I began to enjoy the mix of Jewish, Sicilian, Polish, Black, and Puerto Rican cultures thrown together by economic necessity. Mother thought I shouldn't lower myself by being part of such a mixed crowd. But rebellion chooses its own way in adolescence. "She must be wrong," I thought. I was having so much fun with them, and felt so free, dancing to jukebox hits on the street corner, and learning the latest elephant jokes.

This was a drug-free zone of pure silliness, the carefree play of code words among young people, the delirious nonsense that giddy teenagers used to speak to one another, still pecking away at their shells, desperate to emerge and be counted. These were my peers, for better and for worse. We would all avoid the occasional Gypsy storefront with its beaded curtains and crystal balls. Sultry women in long silken skirts, wearing huge gold-hoop earrings, leaned against the doorway and asked if we wanted our fortunes read. Their dark ways scared us into walking on the outermost edges of the sidewalk, and vowing never to enter their premises. *How could I have guessed then I would one day embrace their occult practices?*

Meanwhile, at home I had won the home prize of the only single bedroom, filling a desperate need for private space in order to survive family tensions. I needed a quiet place to think, and would often get up at three a.m. to do my homework, or study for an exam. One incident stands out in memory that really underlines the effect our home had upon my psyche. It was the one and only tantrum I ever allowed myself to have. One of my brothers had been arguing with my mother, and tensions were mounting. Whatever was said caused me to run from my bedroom and through the house screaming, "stop!" at the top of my lungs, and throwing books and clothes around. The last thing I remember doing was smashing my father's prized shortwave radio. I had become hysterical, and fell sobbing onto my bed.

My mother came in and knelt beside me, stroking my head, crying, and praying. It was a moment of such rare tenderness between us, but at what a price. When my dad came home later on, he forgave me for what I had done, and seemed to understand my outburst had been building for a long time. I had always been a quiet child, having learned to internalize the stress of family life and the many responsibilities heaped upon the firstborn.

Near graduation from high school, a dashing young Czech named Frank dispelled any lure of the nunnery that remained. Mara had introduced us at one of our weekend folk dances. He was witty, intelligent, good-looking, and he was *going places* . . . certainly out of the neighborhood. Frank also disdained the religion of his parents and mine, which intrigued me. Our courtship was simple: we went to the movies, slurped ice-cream sodas through double straws, and ate the popular White Castle hamburgers without onions. Suddenly life's pace had slowed down to a pause at a blinking yellow stoplight. But after winning a New York State scholarship, I decided to go to Hunter College, a liberal and very secular school, a decision that grieved my mother and set off her mental alarm bells.

Frank wanted sexual intimacy soon and promised that marriage would come a little later, after he was established. Besides some moral misgivings, I wasn't emotionally ready to cross that bridge, and only wanted to leapfrog over the slums into the greater halls of learning. "Should we call a four year truce?" he taunted. I didn't understand why he couldn't wait for our friendship to blossom, or why he was pushing me into young adulthood. So I wasn't prepared for the final separation when it did happen. The evening after we said goodbye, I lay crumpled into a sobbing heap on my bed, sweetly comforted by my brothers. "Shall we kill him?" they asked, brandishing Dad's Samurai sword above me. Their sudden switch to chivalry made me laugh between sobs. With that laugh, I had already begun to take mental steps away from the arms of my first love. It was clear he had abandoned me for the thrills of sex and the sweet smell of Madison Avenue success.

Graduation from high school in 1955 took place on two levels for me. White-capped and gowned with my senior class, I marched out from our school auditorium, past the Waldorf Astoria, from Lexington Avenue to Fifth Avenue. We entered this neo-gothic Cathedral named after St. Patrick, about whom I knew nothing. The buttressed ceiling arched high above us, the golden altar gleamed down the great distance of the aisle, and the powerful music of the pipe organ vibrated the wooden pews as it bellowed out our processional. It had become my private chapel for a few hours that day, and my family sat as honored guests waiting for my name to be called, one of four hundred others. With scroll in hand, I took leave of school and the church of my childhood. It was done in secret because of my mother's terrifying allegiance to the faith of her Irish forebears.

Afterward there was a small reception at our home. Dad had stayed behind to prepare the food and lean into his beer. He was in a dancing mood when we arrived. His firstborn had graduated from high school, and was going on to college! He became giddy with pride and boasted about my academic success. Soon the living room was crowded with friends dancing to "Earth Angel" and "The Great Pretender," music provided by 45 rpm records stacked on a small red record player. Frank came, dressed in a suit and tie, and looking very much like a Madison Avenue man. Mother was thrilled to see him, Dad was happily drunk and spouted incoherent compliments, but I was torn apart. We danced once but made no plans to see each other again. Externally, I looked grownup enough to handle losing my first serious boyfriend. I wore a sophisticated black sheath dress and high heels, and my hair was still in the razor-cut French *gamine* style, but my heart trembled like a wounded child.

My grim-lipped spinster Aunt Mary came with her brownie camera as always and took the only pictures we ever had of any notable event. We never thought it necessary to own a camera and depended on her showing up. She asked me about my future plans and if I was going to marry soon. I told her that marriage didn't interest me at all. She was shocked and said, "Don't you want to have a big family like your mother?" Horrified by the years of Mother's thankless toil and drudgery, my response was blunt and cold-blooded. "I don't intend to be an Irish cow." The words rushed out, spilling over the dam of my tongue, unprotected by any virtue of kindness. It was a harsh indictment of the cultural morass of Irish Catholicism that almost killed my mother. I don't doubt that Aunt Mary may have repeated my words as a reprimand to my mother for holding me up as a role model before my sisters, whom I suspected secretly despised me for it. Aunt Mary and I hardly ever spoke again.

We had really connected only once in my childhood when she took me to an upscale parlor with a sign that posed a question, "What does your future hold?" The lady there said she could read the tea leaves left in our cups. It seemed so silly to me then, until I found out that Aunt Mary had lost the one and only love of her life through a fatal accident. Her faith in a loving God had been shaken. I remember seeing her read the daily horoscope column, and wondered if she really believed it could help her. Whenever I questioned her about it she had no real answers.

My old school chum Mara danced me through this first emotional vale of tears caused by my breakup with Frank. I continued the dull high school job of filing annulment records, baptisms, and dispensations in a small clerical office. This meager salary allowed me to buy cigarettes, some new clothes and things I needed for college. The stifling heat of that summer drove me further into the doldrums, and obliterated any joyful memory that remained of the dead-in-the-water relationship.

Chapter Five

An Entrance to Bohemia

Only a few stops further on the subway from Cathedral High School, Hunter College lay far across the chasm from Catholicism. It was a liberal wall-less mix of free-floating minds, not bothering too much about touching solid ground. As I walked up the Sixty-Eighth Street ramp to the school entrance, trying not to panic, I felt like a little "know-nothing" who had somehow wormed her way underground into an elite intelligentsia, and just crossed over a boundary into an unknown world.

For the next four years my soul exploded in all directions. Being branded a heretic hadn't been able to shake my allegiance to Jesus. You might say I was God-haunted, burdened by the enigmas of theology, and "Who was Who" in the God department. My ignorance shamed me; my innocence mocked me; my lust for knowledge alarmed me . . . and soon my iniquities would overtake me. Sororities competed for the bodies of incoming freshman like shoe salesmen, hawking the magic Cinderella-fit for us peasants. I replied, "No, thank you!" as they shouted all their hoopla. There were enough social hurdles ahead of me without adding another rite of passage. Soon I was happily enmeshed in a co-ed gathering of brainiacs and iconoclasts.

When Allen Ginsberg read his recently published poem "Howl" to us in the student lounge, we sat stunned by his gut-wrenching tirade. He painted startling images of a drug-crazed, sex-crazed generation who had rejected everything normal society was offering them and had gone mad in their search for an alternate reality. My concept of poetry—its language and its power—was radically changed that day. Alexander Calder, the maker of whimsical mobiles, headed the Art department, but it was Jackson Pollock who dominated the scene then with his shotgun-paint style canvasses. René Fülöp-Miller, a renowned professor in his field, taught my class in Anthropology, and offered to mentor me after he read my paper on Huxley's *Brave New World*. Not knowing who I was, or what I should do with my life, I turned down his offer. Listening to Jacques Maritain's lectures on Philosophy enlarged my soul and brought momentary enlightenment. All this was a heady cocktail indeed, and I drank it to the dregs.

My new Geometry teacher smoked cigarettes in a short black holder that she bit nervously and moved across her unpainted lips. Her long golden hair was sleeked back and lashed into a ponytail. I approached her cautiously with my plea, "Can you help me learn this stuff? It just doesn't make sense, and two nuns have tried without success!" I explained that my diploma had been given on the condition of passing her course. This dear lady helped me over my first hurdle. Perhaps it was a personal challenge for her to outdo two Dominican nuns, but I somehow got an A in her evening class. She definitely became my personal poster child for the bohemian culture. My disenfranchised soul soon began to speak their language, even though our wars were being fought on different fronts: mine on theological grounds, and theirs on philosophical and sociological grounds.

"Beatniks" were the bearded longhairs who walked the city streets and the halls of higher learning, dressed in torn jeans and sandals. They were called the "Holy Barbarians," by some and also labeled the "do-nothing bohemians" by others. In response, these self-styled "hipsters" had earlier labeled people in conventional society as "squares," because they saw them locked inside little ticky-tacky boxes of boring repetitive norms, and dismissed them as the soulless *bourgeoisie*. This new "Beat Generation" behaved like their predecessors: those bohemians who hid behind dark glasses, drank cheap wine, smoked joints, hung out in Greenwich Village coffee shops and endured the stonewalled complacency and self-righteous stares of middle-class Americans.

Along these fault lines, the plates of societal values would be shifted and shaken for almost thirty years. New shorelines would be uncovered, roots exposed, ancient boundaries buried, foundations crumbled, and innocence quietly stolen. A brutal soul-searching light had been turned on, violating both the public and private spheres, probing and questioning the dusty corners of atrophied scholastic minds. Jean Paul Sartre's question, "What does it all mean?" became a catchall phrase we discussed in our coffee shops and our classrooms.

It seemed good to me then, all of this uproar and upheaval. These social outcasts seemed to possess that mystical quality I craved called "passion." The same hunger gnawed at their viscera and the same thirst desiccated their souls. There were no heroes among them, just angry tattered youth bunched together, some who were wanderers, some who ranted and raved about their inner journeys, and some who painted surreal landscapes of their dreams. They wailed and mourned through the horns of John Coltrane and Miles Davis. They rocked to the melancholy blues of Thelonious Monk's piano.

Yet they all seemed familiar to me: like a Francis of Assisi, who stripped himself of earthly riches, like a Jesus who overturned the money changers' tables, like a Savonarola who cried out in the public square against corruption, like a Joan of Arc—who heard angelic voices, took up armor and the sword to defend her country, but was burned at the stake for sorcery because she cut off her hair and wore male clothing in obedience to God.

"What did I learn in college?" I became, like so many I knew, an educated fool. Yes, I perfected my French to a certain degree of savoir-faire. A few daring friends and I would go to French restaurants dressed all in black, and smoke cigarettes in long holders, hoping to convince the waiters we might be *Rive Gauche* Parisians or avant-garde students on a holiday. By that time I had landed a coveted evening job shelving books at the Main Library on Fifth Avenue and Forty-Second Street that earned me a decent amount of "mad money." The flotsam of student friends in which I floated thickened and thinned with the changing tides. But I could not avoid meeting Frank's old girlfriend, who regaled me with stories of their freshly revived affair and played darts with my heart. I was thankful for Mara who still anchored me to the 'hood, where we slowly exchanged the soda store days for nights at a local bar protected by the Italian Mafia who loved to bet the horses, and yet seemed to be ignored by the local police.

It was there I learned to drink scotch with beer chasers, smoke cigars on a bet, and receive money to light votive candles for superstitious guilt-ridden philanderers, all the while preserving my virginity. This fact so impressed the locals that they put a hand over the hidden gun in their suit pocket and swore to kill anyone who bothered me. The iniquities of my father began to overtake me, and I drank to the point of getting sick. Vomiting out the poison became a new early-morning ritual. At times I would walk home alone, creating a tough image with lighted cigarette in hand to ward off stalkers, then crawl into bed, head spinning and stomach churning.

One evening my charade didn't work. Someone followed me home into the project, and pushed me down onto the grass. His eyes were fiery red with drugs, as he swore at me in Spanish while holding a knife before my eyes. My screams alerted a woman who saw us from the third floor window. And her screams for the police lifted him off me. He ran, while she continued yelling and then asked if I was okay. I couldn't answer her because he had been choking me. I staggered home silently, shaking from fear. My angel had protected me from the horror of rape and possibly even death. It was certainly another undeserved mercy. There were bruises on my throat to remind me of my narrow escape, and I hid them from the family. This was the last time I ever walked home alone.

Soon our visits to the bar became less and less frequent. Mara had fallen in love with a tenderhearted, charming but married bartender. Her stories of their escapades worried me. I knew she was caught like a bird, strapped to the neighborhood perch. That was not what I wanted, though a handsome *Siciliano* had attracted me for a season. Tales of his neighborhood conquests had preceded our meeting and intrigued me enough to write a short story called "The Little Boy Man" and purge my soul of his attempts to sexually ensnare me. My English teacher, a sweet Georgia gal, loved it and was the first one who ever encouraged me in writing.

During my first year at Hunter an ever-widening world of art began to pervade my senses, but nearly cost me my scholarship. Savvy friends introduced me to classic silent films like *The Passion of Joan of Arc*, Eisenstein's *Battleship Potemkin* and Cecile B. DeMille's *King of Kings*. We had to see all the new Japanese films with their breathtaking color landscapes and costumes, and couldn't miss the first of Ingmar Bergman's hauntingly beautiful black and white films like *The Virgin Spring* and *The Seventh Seal*. We had to skip classes to do this. Then we hung out at the Museum of Modern Art, the Guggenheim Museum, and Carnegie Hall. The word *classical* had taken on real meaning, especially in the linguistic world. Latin poetry and essays, Greek dramas and mythology, reading *The Iliad* and *The Odyssey*, and French poetry and novels filled my pauper's cup with the well-aged wines of antiquity. These all taught me to revere the past, heed the wisdom of ancient voices, and to remember that the human drama doesn't change though empires rise and fall, and languages exchange meanings.

My comeuppance finally arrived in the form of being abruptly called into the Dean of Women's office. She asked me why my grade average was a C minus, and what I was going to do about it. How could I dare describe the richness of the education I was receiving outside the classroom? Instead, I knew I was cornered and promised to take extra classes in the summer and evenings to bring up my average. I was off the hook for three more years, but still meandered through the syllabus looking for a focal point. I finally settled on Creative Writing as my major with a minor in Humanities and Languages. Hunter's payback for my extracurricular larks was the loss of course credit in poorly attended classes no matter what grade I had received. My sentence became clearly irrevocable when I realized that I wasn't going to graduate in four years. In effect, my punishment was losing one whole year's credit toward a degree. *It would take me until thirty-seven years later to reverse that judgment. But that's another story.*

Time in New York was winding down to a finish. I had successfully avoided marriage to a Jewish Columbia University pre-med student, and a charming Swedish friend of my brother Charles. A circle of three close-knit school friends and I were busy finalizing our escape plans. Marge, an ambitious, sharp-witted Irish-American cutie; Joan, an intensely serious Jewish would-be ice princess; Joanie, a shy, brilliant Irish lassie plagued by pimples and scruples; and I had all banded together in the cafeteria. Marge had helped me get my plum job at the Main Public Library on Fifth Avenue, and we spent many an evening shelving books and flirting with our supervisor, a bearded Irish professor who distilled his own alcohol on the job. She often brought me home to her Bronx apartment after work, where she and her poetic sister Maureen, a Hunter graduate, lived a quietly bohemian lifestyle under the unsuspecting nose of their simple widowed mother.

Maureen moved like a slender nervous gazelle and spoke in rapture about the poetry of Wallace Stevens. Her Jewish boyfriend, who looked like a huge Russian bear, was a gifted painter. We visited his loft studio, filled with canvasses, mattresses, paints, and wooden palettes. It reeked of beer, cigarettes, pigments, and turpentine. Marge and I engaged in philosophical blathering while his large intense eyes gazed in wonder at Maureen, his beloved hummingbird. He had a Greek friend named Aldo who thought I was Athena incarnate. He invited me to a Greek café and titillated me with wine and sensual music, accompanied by belly dancing, all to no avail. My heart was rigid with an unnamed fear, encased in its own virginal membrane, and I couldn't be pulled away from the vision of an unspoken destiny. The cracker-jack glamour of New York culture—its "excelsior" mentality, the tough-minded sophistication of the "Big Apple," the allure of living at the World's Gate, guarded by the green Goddess of Liberty, whose torch burns with hope for so many wanderers and seekers—had failed to sweep me off course.

Princess Joan had managed to form a singing trio with Marge and me. We harmonized all the popular songs, until she finally arranged a recording session for us to sing her new rockabilly song, called "Cinderella, It's Midnight." We actually cut a 45 rpm record that was sent to various DJs before it fizzled out. Our parents were elated by the thought we might finally become moneymakers. Joan was devastated and decided to stay in New York, still hoping for some hidden glories she might find on the ice rink. As an only child of immigrant parents, she had been sprinkled with the stardust of the *American Dream*, and she was riding hard to catch the golden ring at some turn in life. Joan was so unique in her looks and mannerisms that she could convince anyone by the intensity of her words, especially when they were punctuated by her flashing smile and perfectly white teeth. We had gone along for one of her rides, and had a blast.

Chapter Six

Escaping the Colossus

Before Joan there had been another one-of-a-kind college chum. Leila had come from the other side of the tracks. Her parents were Connecticut professionals who kept an upscale apartment in Manhattan. There they hid their brilliant, love-starved daughter, holding her captive while they pursued a socially demanding lifestyle. Her lonely soul cleaved to mine, and she often begged me to accompany her home. Finally I agreed, and a uniformed doorman bowed to us as we entered the white-stoned building. I followed her to the elevator and gasped when she unlocked the door to a huge black and white tiled hallway that led to a windowed world of elegant furniture and paintings.

At first, my innocence didn't allow me to interpret her signals as an invitation to have a lesbian relationship. I can remember only my emotional recoil at any advance. Once while we were chatting around the unease, we heard a key beginning to unlock the front door. She quickly shoved me into her bedroom closet and greeted her mother with an arch sweetness. Their exchange sickened me: the quasi-British pomp of her mother's voice against the lackeyed murmuring of my cornered friend's response. Then it shifted into an investigation regarding her social life. Leila became a defendant and her mother, the judge and accuser. Finally the question came, "Have you been hobnobbing again with the garbage man's daughter?

Haven't we asked you not to do that?" As I hid in the darkness of that closet, I felt betrayed. Her mother finally left in anger, late for a cocktail date. Leila soon released me, her invisible verboten friend, into the raw light that now defined our friendship.

Her mother's perfume hung between us like a veil. Leila knew that her mother's words had stabbed me, and comforted me with cookies and milk. Somehow her words had an opposite effect on me, and cured me of any longing for the brassy glitz of wealth. The empty trappings of Leila's life no longer held me in thralldom. As an only child, she was raised to pursue a career in medicine but lacked the drive and *savoir faire* it required. Her parents couldn't hide their disappointment in her. She was definitely another wounded bird. In their eyes she had crossed her blue-blood lines into a society of the unwashed. She never again invited me to her apartment, but instead I took her home with me where she found real acceptance, enjoying simple meals and teatime around our table. She flirted with my brother Charles, hugged my mother's apron-wrapped body and danced with my beer-breathy father. He did in fact drive a tugboat down the East River that hauled garbage headed for the Atlantic dump. I was no longer ashamed of being his daughter. After college, life carried her to a different port of destiny, and we never saw each other again.

Another thing to understand is that I was unable to form real attachments in those days. Everything was in flux, in movements away from and into lives, without ever being touched or touching anyone. It was fully experimental, like trying on different clothes and seeing that nothing really fit well. Since we aren't made to see ourselves, we depend on mirrors; the hard ones of molten sand, and the softer ones of loving friends. Through them we hope to catch the truest image of ourselves. But there are distortions in both, because we are all exposed to the same scrutiny of light waves that reflect us to one another. Our brains, like the cameras we have developed, record all the lights and shadows of our days imprinted on memory cells. In the computer world a virus can eat up banks of random memory and crash whole systems into nano dust. In our flesh and blood world, minds can be invaded with a chemical virus and suddenly become vacant, memories erased, identities confused, and time distorted. The complexity of our daily human drama doesn't need another deus ex machina *to appear and win the day, nor a* deus ex homine *to control it, but a* Deus Incarnatus *to redeem it.*

During my high school days I had once read a newspaper article about a government-sponsored land rush to Alaska. I was excited enough to call the family into a meeting, and showed them the facts. Here was our chance to own property, to be homesteaders, and be like pioneers! We could fill our lungs with fresh air, refresh our eyes with lush natural beauty, and put our hands to the plough. Sadly, there were no takers. Not even my farm-girl mother could be stirred from her nest. I remember thinking "This is our way out!" But they probably looked at me, and thought, *"The way out of what? Hadn't the cosmos been crystallized inside the New York harbor?"*

My family didn't feel trapped in New York's grinding treadmill of streets, subways, and cars, or feel oppressed by the daily crush of people. Although they were encased in concrete canyons, they still enjoyed the spinning top, the whirligig world of constant motion. I felt like a changeling living in their midst. And so, after tasting the Big Apple for some twenty years, it was time for me to travel on. Marge had encouraged me to go with her to the University of California Berkeley (UCB) and pursue a Master's degree in Library Science. It seemed a respectable goal to my parents, and permission to leave home was easily granted. Genius Joanie joined us, only with the proviso of our carefree protection, and seemed to relish the adventure as much as we did.

Leaving New York was not the burning issue, but leaving my dear dysfunctional family was. It was going to be a knife-edged moment. Mother had taken weeks to come by boat to Canada from Ireland, and then days by train to New York. Dad's parents had sailed for months from Germany to New York's Ellis Island. In one generation, their oldest daughter could fly from East Coast to West by airplane in a relatively few hours. Joanie, Marge, and I climbed aboard, and buckled down into our first airplane ride, heading out to California, God's Country, our promised land. The tiny oval window framed the faces of our families waving goodbye as the plane shook and thrust us from the sucking pull of the runway. We held onto fragile armrests, belted against the sky, tearing into clouds that seemed painted onto a blue ceiling. Everything we knew slowly vanished from sight, until we could no longer identify place or time. The separation from this early lifetime nearly severed my soul from my body. Voiceless sobs pushed me down into the tiny pillow. This was pain for which there had been no preparation.

They were suddenly all gone from me: Charles, the chess-playing intellectual; Johnny, the love-struck sailor who would marry Eileen, his high school sweetheart; Eddy, the prince of bowling alleys; Margaret, the charming child, now grown into a blonde babe; Susan, the tender-hearted one; Kathleen, the gypsy princess and newly-minted Daddy's girl; and Bernadette Rose, the fragile skin and bone replica of an earlier me. She was the one I pleaded with my mother to let me bring along with me. But why was I going into the wild blue yonder, God knows where, and alone? My fractured family, the funny hometown rowdies and the school circle of crazies were being washed away in shameless tears. The droning engines lulled me to sleep and numbed the pain.

The book I brought along to read sent a chilling message to my heart. Caitlyn Thomas had written a memoir called *Leftover Life to Kill*, about the turbulent relationship she had with her deceased husband, the famous Welsh poet, Dylan Thomas. The story was a jumble of self-purging portraits, edged with anger and laced with bittersweet moments of a hapless love that nearly drowned her in self-pity. But somehow we both were asking the same question: she, an artist's widow fighting for her right to live again, and me, a tenderfoot virgin on life's shoreline, playing with the sands of time. *What would become of our lives now? Was life laid out on a table in uneven portions, a feast for some, and for others, a sorry meal of leftovers?* I resolved not to let the passage of time bury me in a slow death.

My role model then was George Sand, a French novelist, who challenged the cultural milieu of her time, and dared to "keep company" with men. This nineteenth century bohemian was trapped inside a female body, and used a masculine pen name to publish her books. I identified with her flamboyant nature, her creative ability and her fearless stance to be treated as an artistic equal in a man's world. Time had not yet become a treasure, so I carelessly kicked at it, let it run through my fingers, like the prodigal I was. Admittedly a romantic, believing that good would always triumph over evil, and beauty would ultimately flourish in earth's most barren places, I dared to dream that my lackluster life could be resurrected from the dry bones of my beginnings.

PART TWO: BERKELEY

Battleground for New Beginnings

"Look, I go forward, but He is not there, and backward, but I cannot perceive Him; When He works on the left hand, I cannot behold Him; when He turns to the right hand, I cannot see Him."
(Job 23: 8–9 NKJV)

California became the place where I fully experienced both the beauty and power of Nature for the first time. I came to understand how mountains could become magnets, pulling us upwards by the sheer thrill of ascension. Crowning the earth with their grandeur, they challenge us to drink an elixir of the gods, attain to divine heights, and place our feet in triumph upon their necks. Dazed by gaining such a glorious panorama, for a brief moment we stand as lords of the earth. Our souls expand along with our lungs, and this greater breathing room feeds a new fire. Seeds of great potential burst open in the heat of it all, and we long to live in this higher dimension forever. So many people have given their lives and their fortunes in exchange to be part of this triumphal procession.

Mt. Everest, the mother of all mountains, has yielded her neck to many a frail human creature carrying within the Imago Dei, and the promise of dominion over the earth. Mt. Whitney, in the California Sierras, was the first one to fall beneath my feet. Trying to climb it with some daredevil friends in just one day almost caused me to sleepwalk off a cliff. Luckily someone had a flashlight and saw the edge before it was too late. The otherworldly majesty of those granite peaks had inspired me but my own limitations had sufficiently humbled me.

Many years later, my husband John, daughter Aimée, and I climbed the snow-covered Mt. Shasta, a solitary beauty rising above the western plains, and that expedition finally slaked my thirst for conquering mountains. But that's another story.

California possesses a rich variety of landscapes in which to play at life: rivers to raft, deserts to wander, forests to explore, caves to descend, mountains to ascend, snowy slopes to ski, waves to surf and beaches to walk. I had entered an immense doorway through which to view a portion of earth's glories. From such a vista, New York City, the cradle of my childhood, seemed like a polyglot wasteland, festering with sores from garbage-strewn ghettos, gangs carving out their turfs, drug alleys and barren, treeless streets. I felt fortunate to have escaped, but was guilt-ridden nonetheless for having done so.

Chapter One

The Great Disconnect

In August of 1959, three eager hatchlings landed in Berkeley, California, in time to celebrate my twenty-second birthday. We were quite unconscious of our Yankee ways: the strut and stride we had acquired racing across streets to avoid taxis and to catch trains and buses, the shotgun speed of "*r*-less" speech that pummeled people when we asked for directions. Our "c'mon already!" attitude met the great Western wall of American grit, as we hit the ground in a dead run. New Yorkers usually develop a fast walk that leaves others breathless. It's the "places to go, people to see, out of my way" pace. Slowing down at all is not to be endured, and can even be suicidal when navigating taxi-dominated traffic.

"Hey, Marge, check her out," I said, as we boarded a bus driven by a large muscular woman, who bit her lips into a cutesy smile as we stared at our first lady pioneer. Instead of a bonnet and apron, she wore trousers and uniform; instead of a six-gun and holster, she wore a leather money belt. "So this is what became of women after the West was won," I thought. Suddenly we were "dudesses" in a new wilderness. When we stopped for coffee at a local drugstore, I overheard a man ordering a bear claw, and waited awestruck, for the waitress to serve it. She brought out a sugar-swabbed pastry on a plate, to my dumb-founded amazement. I stuck my greenhorn foot even further in my mouth and asked, "Do you have any egg creams?" She looked puzzled and asked, "No, hon, what're they?" Then I had felt it my duty to educate her and explain how to make the famous New York cocktail with seltzer water, milk, and chocolate syrup. Her eyebrows tilted up, her head turned slowly sideways, and she said, "Sorry hon, wanna Pepsi?" These were the first East meets West tremors that immersed us in a mild culture shock.

The hustle of the first days in motels ended abruptly when we rented a house in a quiet, clean neighborhood shaded by elm trees. We were almost traumatized by the silence, the cleanliness, but mostly by the lack of people and garbage on the streets. A lonely professor at UCB lived next door to us. He was waiting for his wife to join him, and relished being entertained by our giggling female company. He kindly invited us to a spaghetti dinner at his place, tried to make sense of our staccato-style questions, and briefed us on the steps we had to take in order to become students. First, we had to establish residency and that would take a year. Then we could apply for a student loan from the government. It was a very pleasant orientation, replete with maps of the city, and transportation tips. We ended the evening merrily lifting up our wine glasses to a successful future.

All I could think about was how close we were to San Francisco. This had become the new home of the "beatniks." I had heard that Kerouac, Ferlinghetti, and Allen Ginsburg gave poetry readings at coffee houses. That rumor swiveled my soul's direction as I searched the ads for a job. An insurance company downtown hired me, as I had plenty of clerical experience and had worked at the famous library on Forty-Second Street and Fifth Avenue. My funny speech and serious demeanor might have intrigued them as well. The truth was that I was on a manhunt. All I wanted then was to catch a glimpse of those "Holy Barbarians" who might still be hiding somewhere in the city's dense caverns. The bus ride over the Bay Bridge was actually enjoyable. Everything seemed cleaner, everyone moved much slower, but the city scene soon reeked of boredom. Even the California speech pattern was non-accented and blah, and I vowed I would never let it pollute the Eastern dialect I had perfected: a cross between my mother's brogue, and my father's Bronx bark. My melded speech was often mistaken for a British accent, which I found hilarious. *As fate would have it, one generation later I perfected that exact form of speech, spawned by Hollywood speech teachers and now considered the perfect vehicle (rather than the once preferred British accent) for teaching English as a second language.*

Magnetic Marge found a job at the local public library and made some interesting new friends. Genius Joan found some employment at an old bookstore. Soon the three of us were initiated into the ritual of eating a locally grown thistle called artichoke. We sat cross-legged on the floor, scraping our teeth over tasteless leaves, until we reached its heart. That evening we toasted the beginning of all my Berkeley *non compos mentis* moments with cheap Chianti, and the taste chase began for all things Mexican: guacamole, salsa, tacos, tortillas, enchiladas, and chile rellenos.

Her fellow librarians also took us on a tour of Yosemite Valley, and we all stayed in a cabin as the first snows fell during Christmas Break. My eyes ached, as I looked upwards, stunned by a pure beauty, untouched by man, something I had never seen before. Then I understood why I had traded the concrete monoliths of New York for this primal grey magnificence that sparkled with ice, etched in feathery trails of snow. White bone-chilling water gushed out of dark rocks and canyons and made a ceaseless roar. My every muscle strained upward in awe at a sky overflowing with endless stars. One evening, I started to climb up some jagged boulders in my ballet slippers. Wine had warmed and emboldened me. It didn't feel odd to be without gloves, hat, or boots. My friends were laughing at my sudden frenzy to climb, but called me back before I made a serious misstep.

Meanwhile, I had to navigate life on a manmade mountain, a building that towered some twenty stories, dedicated to the repossessing of houses and cars, taken from those who had failed to make payments. My boss was a lovely woman named Frances, who endured a clinical relationship with a dull doctor husband at home and savored a butch girlfriend at the office. These two showed me around the lesbian haunts. I was fascinated by these wild shadow shows of women, cock-walking along the trail of "femmes" languishing at the bar. This was a miniature *Forbidden City*, oozing with raw insinuations, driven by sexual needs and humming with head-turning remarks about body parts. Fran tried to persuade me of her right to get what she needed there. But deep down inside she knew that she was trading what may have been a humdrum marriage with a future for momentary cheap thrills. She must have thought I was a queer duck, just sitting there and pitying these poor women. And she laughed when I told her that what I feared most about being in San Francisco were earthquakes. When one actually hit, she calmly told me, "Don't worry sweetie; this building's on rollers!" I could hardly breathe as everything swayed for eternal seconds. I held on to the doorway and watched the desks roll back and forth, thankful that it stopped as quickly as it began.

As a child, I remembered crawling on the pavement to push against the hurricane winds that swept across the Eastern seaboard. I had early learned to respect the forces of lightning and thunder, shuddering under the wrathful sounds from heaven. But now, to feel the earth beneath me shift away, the familiar pull of gravity suspended, birthed a newborn fear. There was nowhere to stand, except between doorposts, or to hide under something that wouldn't move, and wait it out. Fran watched my terror with amusement. California was supposedly God's Country, but riddled with a fatal flaw. *Had I been drawn to the edge of some fragile frontier that someday might be sheared off, set adrift in the Pacific, or become another sunken hulk like Atlantis? Was there any place safe enough to begin a new life?*

Berkeley's college town charm soon assuaged my fears, and I began to enjoy the interesting mix of professorial talking heads and the gathering masses of liberal, radical students. They met together around marble tables, endlessly conversing and smoking, their rising crescendo of voices in the Mediterraneum, the iconic Italian coffee house on Telegraph Avenue. Because my mother had preached McCarthyism and John Birch's philosophy from her bully pulpit, I had vigorously re-programmed my brain to distrust anyone's political stance. I was convinced that Literature, Music, and the Arts could transcend the status quo and never be servile to the machinations of power mongers. They were the only free agents destined to disburse and preserve the best of human expression. However, this would prove to be a slippery slope later on when psychedelic drugs came into play. Soon my year as an "indentured servant" came to an end, and I happily said goodbye to Fran and her strange coterie.

San Francisco never yielded the bohemian icons I sought. Maybe they were hiding in an insane asylum with Kesey, or *On the Road* again with Kerouac. It was time to be a student again, so I gave up chasing my dreams of any life-changing encounters. Marge had found a black boyfriend with an Oriental persona. He taught us how to play goh, drink saki, and appreciate taekwondo. He was a gently buffed-out giant who nonchalantly wore his black belt. Marge and I rarely saw each other from then on. Genius Joan proved to be too fragile for this transition and had escaped from our experimental compound to rejoin the more familiar madness of New York City.

The political climate was changing rapidly as I stepped onto the Berkeley campus. The decade of the 60s had rolled in with cyclonic force, fueled by revolutionary foment. Che Guevara was the man of the hour, and of course, Fidel Castro. Their pictures and slogans were everywhere. These revolutionary leaders of angry young men were like the unpredictable rogue waves that seemed to come out of nowhere, and threatened to swallow up the destinies of a whole generation. The air was thick with social protests, but I was both ignorant of their consequences and undeterred in my small quest for a place in the sun. So I signed on many a dotted line, enrolled in prestigious courses, secured a college loan, bought the many required texts, and answered an ad for a room to rent. My disconnection to the cosmos was about to become cavernous.

The house on Prince Street looked like a Swiss chalet, shaded by giant elm trees on the outside. The living room boasted a black grand player piano, lofty exposed beams, and a huge brick fireplace. My room was small, but fit my budget well, and even came with a part-time job. The owner's daughter Leslie showed me around. She was an exquisitely beautiful teenager with dream-white skin, sparkling clear blue eyes and curly red-blonde hair. Her mother, Kitty, owned a restaurant nearby and said I could work there for tips and good meals. The rental situation fit me like a glove, and was within walking distance to the university. I had never lived in such a lovely home and felt like a gypsy princess. But the house on Prince Street gave me more than a place to stay: it changed my destiny.

Chapter Two

Tuning In

The excitement of entering such a prestigious university propelled me into a studied frenzy of buying books, navigating buildings and classrooms, and reading maps. I needed to understand the vast array of curriculum and the rules of engagement for each professor's syllabus. Berkeley campus had an old-world charm coupled with a very dignified air. There were many grassy areas and benches under large green trees. While those should have been an invitation to relax, make new friends, and enjoy the scenic beauty, I couldn't slow down enough. Marge and I met often in the cafeteria to compare notes. She seemed to relish the challenges and was adjusting well to university life. I quickly assessed that the math required in Astronomy was too difficult and dropped the class. Just being one of so many thousands of students was overwhelming. But I had crafted a two-year life plan: first, to complete my undergraduate credits lost because of poor class attendance, and second, to apply for a Masters in Library Science. My instincts warned me I might be swimming in waters way over my head.

The small rented room was cell-like, and located immediately off the huge kitchen and dining room. I placed a picture of Jesus on a desk that looked out onto a lovely backyard. Leslie brought me over to meet her mother Kitty who owned the restaurant that bore her name, and I ate my first meal there. The food was delicious, and

Kitty quickly scooped me up into her world. Soon I was waiting tables, and learning how to cook. Hilda, the main chef, was a hard-working German lady who kept things in order, and also had a great sense of humor. Her laughter was like an engine that kept the kitchen humming. Esther, a gracious southern gal with a bohemian bent (she liked to take air baths) was another cook, who specialized in desserts. I sensed a new destiny emerging as I took my part in this interesting family, and I really enjoyed serving the public, learning a new skill, and earning good tips.

As we sat together after the dinner rush waiting for the last customers who lingered, I gradually realized that Kitty was so much more than a short order cook. She was a lioness, a hard-working single mother by choice, who taught special needs children during the day and managed her restaurant by night. After three failed marriages, she had learned to blur the hard edges of life with wine. Cigarettes and alcohol were eating away at her full-bosomed beauty. She exuded the soul strength of powerful convictions like my own mother, but of the opposite persuasion, and introduced me to the other side of the political coin. This was a woman whose educated brilliance once concluded that God was dead, and that Marxist philosophy held the only sensible cure for society's ills. She and her first husband Raymond had worked to organize labor unions, and championed the rights of the oppressed, whether white or black. Like many of her generation, she had to endure being blackballed and socially ostracized for her stance. I admired her convictions and her intellect tremendously, and felt honored to work for her. She had much to teach me besides how to cook.

Leslie was getting used to having me around the house. At first she confessed that she didn't like me because I was too nervous and intense. And because of her quiet devotion as her mother's caretaker, and surrogate homemaker, I hardly noticed her presence at first. Whenever she spoke about Kitty it was clear how much she valued her mother's sacrifices to keep their beautiful home, and provide for them as a family. Soon I met another daughter named Abbie, who showed up to work some evenings at the restaurant. She was vibrancy personified, drop-dead gorgeous, and spoke English with a mixed black southern-British clip. Her lack of vanity and her sheer enjoyment of people delighted me. She seemed fully *Alive* with a capital A, and I felt twinges of envy watching her screw up her face, or cross her eyes in comic relief, to get her point across. Working next to her, I felt so wooden, so weighted down by an indefinable feeling I had learned from reading German romantics. They called it *Weltschmertz*, or "world pain," a sadness or oppression caused by perceiving the contrast between the real world and the ideal world.

This recent high school graduate was such a confident young woman of the world; whereas, I was an introverted, artsy college student who felt like a displaced innocent abroad. To my surprise, we became fast friends and still are to this day. At one point she even joined Marge, Joanie, and me, packed like sardines in the small yellow VW Marge had bought from her boyfriend *Jimbo*, on a cross-country trip. Since I was a non-driver, they appointed me as the "gazetteer," to read the road maps for direction as we traveled. She and Marge took turns driving us three thousand miles to New York City, where she met my family, and even lived with them for a while before pursuing her own dreams there. The occasion for my brief return was my cousin Margaret's wedding. *How could I know I wouldn't see the streets of New York ever again, or my parents for another twenty years!* I remember how shocked I was to see that my mother's hair had turned completely white, but my family seemed otherwise unchanged. I felt even more like a stranger in their midst, and was eager to resume my new life in Berkeley. It was on my return trip to Prince Street that Bernadette was allowed to come and visit. I was eager to introduce her to my new "family" at Kitty's restaurant. I don't remember how long she stayed with us. But nothing in my old life or new life had prepared me for meeting Jeffrey Stewart, Abbie and Leslie's older brother. It would become a turning point in all our lives.

He walked quietly into the dining room, rocking with a deliberate small limp to his steps, and wearing a military-style blue raincoat that exposed a bare chest. Jeff had been raised freeborn, unrestrained, and his sexual powers had ripened early. He sauntered over to the island counter where I was bending over my homework, and unnerved me. His sudden appearance seemed oddly out of place at first in a home that seemed dominated by women. He was a tall, self-conscious hipster, recently home from a jail stint after a drug bust, definitely not shy, but eager to display the masculine power he exerted over the female sex. Jeff had thick curly blonde hair, the same sparkling blue eyes of his siblings, and his lean and tanned body moved easily onto the chair across from me. He spoke with a peculiar Southern accent, similar to his sister Abbie. She could have been his twin in good looks and personality.

He sat opposite me, elbows on the counter, and his thumbs perched under his eyeteeth as he smiled. I could instantly feel the animal warmth of his gaze, as he looked me over. He was obviously used to his effect on women, and enjoyed my nervous confusion as we exchanged names and introductory trivia. I excused myself and went back into my room, sensing this mutual attraction might bring complications I wasn't prepared for, and a new kind of trouble. At the same time, it was a delightful reprieve from the rigid repulsion I experienced being hounded by lesbians. I gradually learned to breathe in the fire he had ignited. We were living in the same house, and the easy-going ambience I had enjoyed before that first encounter was changed in a moment. My relatively simple life as a student was about to end. I had to lean harder into my books with a greater fervency, as classes piled on more homework and tests.

Holy Hubert on Berkeley Campus, circa 1970
courtesy of Robert Dutina

Chapter Three

Turning On

Jeff began to share his struggles in life against the expectations of society, even confessing he had done some jail time. He saw himself as a type of *Spartacus*, a warrior who freed others from slavery, and asked me to read that book which had inspired him, and I did. Soon he got me to leave my hermit shell more often than not. It took courage for me to show him a collection of poems and thoughts I kept in a little blue notebook. I shared my dream of becoming a writer like George Sand. Admittedly I found this smiling *white Negro* fascinating, and feared I was falling in love. We still lived on different planets, so I first had to be initiated into his circle. One evening when we were alone, he rolled up some marijuana and asked me to smoke a joint with him. It seemed like the logical next step in our growing friendship, and I was certainly curious enough. He watched my face alternate between fear, surprise, and wonder. But my first experience sent me literally upward, and I saw myself floating on the ceiling. "So this is what it means to get high," I said, giggling. But I was shaking with both fear and laughter at the same time. He was delighted by my response, and so it became a daily routine with us.

He had effectively turned me on. My soul was loosed from its moorings as I joined his rebel tribe. I had just crossed over the opening of a new frontier. The Berkeley campus became a foreign country that I visited now and then. My disjointed mental state finally forced me to "psych out" of school, and leave the mundane world of academia for the arcane world of a drug-expanded consciousness. I explained that I couldn't cope with the stress of student life any longer, and the office of Registrar assured me that my name would be purged from their academic records, as if I had never been there. Life had just launched me into unfamiliar terrain, and my imagination was thoroughly engaged by the promise of adventure, and the potent smell of danger.

Getting high also caused me to crave cigarettes and liquor, and triggered a growing sexual attraction between us. He brought home some of his mostly black Telegraph Avenue friends who spoke in jive talk and jazz riffs. They were obviously curious to meet this New York gal who had landed on his doorstep and caught his attention. Soon I was invited to join their group for coffee and drug-crazy conversation. They soon elevated me to a position they labeled "too big for the Catholic Church." I was entranced with these jive-talking, dope-smoking social rebels, and was quickly accepted into an underground movement that predated hippies. They had been distancing themselves from the old beatnik cult, those who had formerly rejected the social constraints and mores of normal "straight" society, and had formed a new kind of "hip culture" that embraced rebellion in all its forms.

Berkeley's campus became overrun with demonstrations, and many voices joined with the great cry being raised against injustice demonstrated by the Civil Rights movement and Martin Luther King, Jr. But no one listened to the gentle voice of Holy Hubert who would come every day and preach the Gospel, because he represented the status quo. I watched horrified once as students pelted him with eggs and rotten tomatoes while he tried to tell them about Jesus. Ironically, it was also the time when the free speech movement had begun and Mario Savio, a young philosophy student, rallied his fellow students with these words: "There comes a time when the operation of the machine becomes so odious, makes you so sick at heart, that you can't take part . . . and you've got to put your bodies on the gears, and upon the wheels, upon the levers, upon all the apparatus . . . to make it stop." A growing number of students rebelled against the entrenched academic hierarchy, walked out of classes, and defied their policies that prohibited any political action on campus.

Within six short months I had lost my identity as a student, had lost my virginity, and had become a pothead. The turn-on had been complete. I was infatuated with Jeff and his running after pleasure, his running with the rebels, the dropouts, and the party chasers. I sensed this was madness, but it didn't unnerve me. Everything could still fit nicely into my artist's bag. It was such a turning away from my former self, such a run into darkness, that my own rebellion thrilled me. This outward illicit excitement was what gradually led to sexual intimacy between us. Being ignorant of life's realities, and especially of the power of sex, I gave my virginity to him, carelessly, and without remorse. One strange requirement for us to become an "official" couple was Jeff's insistence that I tear up the picture of Jesus I kept on my desk. Perhaps he instinctively knew this was his only real rival, and I sheepishly complied. In one dark moment I exchanged my childish love relationship with Jesus for a flesh and blood relationship. The memory of that rush of abandonment, of throwing overboard any kind of moral restraints, and my soul's betrayal has haunted me as a constant reminder of human frailty.

Our relationship became apparent to the ladies of the house. Abby was still away in New York but would have been sympathetic; Leslie was still relatively innocent of the affair, but Kitty was furious. She asked me to leave, and admonished me for carrying on with a minor present in the house, her daughter Leslie. She must have thought it was I who had seduced her son, two years younger than me. Leaving the home on Prince St. and my job in Kitty's restaurant began a decade long odyssey of insane wanderings that would take me to the brink of despair and suicide.

Chapter Four

Dropping Out

After borrowing some money from his father Raymond to help start a new life, Jeff found us a small house with an enormous living room that soon became filled with his drug buddies. I easily got a job at the public library since I had met Frank the director a year ago through our mutual friend, Marge. The arrangement was for me to be the breadwinner, and the "square" front of our crazy home life. For five days a week, I dressed in the role of a librarian, and went to work in Squaresville. But on the weekends I enjoyed the drug-fueled freedoms of bohemia. Jeff's powers of persuasion soon developed a thriving business of selling kilos of marijuana. Since buying pieces of furniture was not a priority of our lifestyle, old mattresses on the floor took the place of beds and couches. Hence the term "pad" became synonymous with home. I bought some odd chairs, old rugs and pillows, candles, and odds and ends of kitchenware, all scoured from the local Goodwill store.

Raymond enjoyed visiting to check us out, and often brought us bags of groceries. He was happy to see Jeff setting up house. We enjoyed a brief celebrity status as the new couple on the block. Ralph and Pooh, an older couple expecting their first child came and brought us a record called *Missa Luba* that became the musical background for the constant flow of customers and friends. As an ex-Catholic, I was pleasantly surprised to discover that this was a Mass not sung in Latin, but by an African choir in their native Congolese dialect, using their voices and drums as instruments. Getting high, drinking wine or Southern Comfort, were necessary aids to keep the party pad constantly full of interesting characters. Those "carefree days of wine and roses" changed forever when Jeff came home one day with a bag of sugar cubes laced with LSD. He somehow had joined with a group of volunteers that were paid to try this powerful new drug. Timothy Leary, a wild-eyed Harvard professor had been "turning on" his academic colleagues, and was eager now to share a new means of attaining higher consciousness with the Berkeley faculty. Jeff knew he had scored something extraordinary and was excited to hand out the sugar cubes with a promise that we were going on a fantastic trip. And so, without any warning or prior knowledge of its effects, we all sucked on them that night, waiting for the bright lights of this homemade Nirvana to turn on. Anything but that happened.

Lysergic Acid is a synthesized chemical that produces effects similar to those of mescaline (from the peyote cactus), which is used by American Indians to induce a trance and see visions. These hallucinogens act by disrupting the interaction of nerve cells in the brain and the neurotransmitter serotonin, speeding up or slowing down the transmissions between the neurons, and thus intensifying sensory experiences. There are moments when senses cross over each another and one sees music and hears color. Leary had become the voice of the Great Disconnect with his mantra, "Tune-in, turn-on, and drop-out"! We wanted to be part of these psychedelic pioneers who dared to cross the fragile frontiers of consciousness into unknown vistas of the soul. And so we had unknowingly joined his fallen-angel band. When we dropped acid, we also dropped out of sight, out of mind, and out of all that seemed normal.

The veil had been torn away. My first trip to the inner sphere became a rite of passage into hell. The wine of insanity had been offered to me, but I refused to drink it. My first taste of this brew left me wallowing in a black hole for many years to come. Sitting alone in a corner for hours, I battled to retain what was left of my will. The group around me had obeyed Leary's command to "Let go!" They had entered this uncharted territory of the psyche without fear. But all I could see were people walking around like green skeletons, each shut up in their own private tombs. The horrible visions of that night, the long hours of internal isolation, and the fear of danger from one another's madness, scarred my soul with demonic terror. At one point Jeff came running in to communicate the wonders of his trip, to make love, or to see how I was doing. But I was unreachable, locked into a desperate mental struggle to keep within the boundaries of sanity, and he had no patience with me, and pushed me away with the cold words, "You're no good!" and ran out the door again. Those few words of rejection annihilated me emotionally, and I sat in a catatonic state of withdrawal for a long time, feeling abandoned and left to struggle alone back through the tunnel of time. It took uncountable hours that night for all of us to return to the world of reality.

Months later we heard about other young people drowning in the ocean, thinking they could walk on water. Some had tried to fly out of windows, and some never again returned to sanity. It was shocking to see familiar faces become vacant, and others who mumbled incoherently, who were completely lost in another dimension. They had gone somewhere I didn't want to go, and had become just hollow shells. And Jeff too was gone somewhere I couldn't follow. Given over! Just plain gone! I never really saw the one to whom I had given my virginity again. He became an apostle of the steel drum, hammering out the rhythms of Bacchus. Women smelled sex in his sweat while they danced, and he devoted himself to their hunger for thrills. But I was just as gone from him, having become more like a vestigial appendage, a taunting memory of the world we had known before LSD. We had been joined to this "madding crowd" for better or for worse. We both now lived in another dimension, radically set apart from each other and from normal life.

And so we skipped between the lines of reality and fantasy on Telegraph Avenue, on the outside looking a lot like the aliens we had already become on the inside. The Flower Children generation had just been born, and we participated and perpetuated the image by stealing roses out of a professor's garden, and wearing them as garlands in our hair. Our theme song "This land is your land, this land is our land" certainly meant to include their sidewalk gardens and all their flowers. One loaded sugar cube had nearly shredded my soul, baptized my senses to fever-pitch intensity, and ripped open my mind to explore a cul-de-sac of spiritual vagaries. We seemed to have located the mother lode of all religions. Nirvana was no longer just for religious devotees, but also for the common man. LSD promised to connect all the dots of the inner sanctum.

Or so Leary would have had us believe. He went on to explore further depths of this new higher consciousness, got kicked out of Harvard, and became the high priest of an experimental religious order of dropouts. A new American tribe of longhaired hipsters, now dubbed "hippies," had emerged to peacefully resist the power of the WASP consensus. Their women wore long colorful dresses made of Indian fabric, put flowers in their long hair, draped themselves with lots of handmade jewelry, and declared that sexual love was free, with no skin or strings attached. Their men declared that war was an ancient evil soon to be abolished. The scalding springs of revolution had erupted over the world, and society was being purified from within, but we, as hippies, were seen as the scum that had just surfaced. Meanwhile we took whatever we wanted from huge Safeway dumpsters like scavengers on a hunt for treasures from an ancient sunken boat, and pitied those who stubbornly clung to material possessions.

Then I happily discovered I was pregnant, and enjoyed the new roundness of my body. Our home continued to be the happening place, and the only question that seemed to matter was "Where's the next party, man?" One night after leaving one of these parties, Jeff suddenly knocked me down on the sidewalk, and kicked me hard in the stomach. I was so high and juiced that the physical pain didn't register then. He apparently didn't like the attention I had gotten from his cronies, and flew into a jealous rage. Cheating on him had never occurred to me, though I had plenty of opportunity for a fling or two. His friends shouted profanities at him, grabbed him, and made him stop. But I found out later that he had also pushed my cousin John Francis down and had violently kicked him for fooling around with his younger sister Leslie during a brief stay with me a year earlier on Prince Street.

Ralph's wife Pooh rescued me and took me to the hospital, where the baby was spontaneously aborted. I endured considerable physical pain but the emotional pain of losing this innocent child was unbearable. I sobbed when the nurse announced that I had given birth to a perfectly formed fetus. Instead of asking her whether it was a boy or girl, I asked if she would baptize the baby for me, and she agreed. When the doctor found out, he was so upset with the nurse and me, and said the child did not resemble human tissue. I was completely ignorant of the fact that aborted babies like mine were put into a jar filled with formaldehyde to become specimens, or something much worse. Pooh and I never talked about the baby's fate, even though she had watched everything, and we soon left.

The house was strewn with empty wine bottles, and packed with people as I stumbled through the door, red-eyed with grief. Everyone got quiet as Jeff took my arm and tried to comfort me. "You didn't do anything wrong," he said. "I'm the murderer," he mumbled. My soul shrank from him even though he had been remorseful. Then he helped me lie down across the mattress on the floor. I sank down on it, chained by fear to this man that shared the same guilt I did. How could I even think we had the right to bring a child into this madness? My soul was tormented with self-loathing because I was too weak to run away. LSD had caused me to travel too far too quickly, but I had passed the turnaround point long ago. My new master, Jeff, seemed to wear a smiling death mask, and I continued to cower in the dark corners of my mind in fear of more punishment from him.

Chapter Five

Exit Stage Left

We had moved to a nicer home nearer Telegraph Avenue but our party lifestyle abruptly ended when the police raided our place. I had just come home from the library that afternoon and sat down at the kitchen table to drink a cup of tea. The living room was inhabited by a crazy quilt of people listening to the wailing horn of John Coltrane. Jeff was busy upstairs measuring out kilos of pot to sell. Suddenly, some policemen kicked open the front door. Panic ensued, and people started running out the back door. I sat frozen with fear, quivering inside. Jeff was brought downstairs and handcuffed in front of me. He was seething in anger, and hurled curses at the man who had posed as his business partner, but was actually a paid informant. Looking at me sadly, he told me to tell his mother what had happened. When the house had been cleared, the police released me, and I walked back to Prince Street house alone, still trembling from the violent assault on our lives and the stunning act of betrayal. Leslie called her mother with the news, and they let me stay there out of pity for our predicament. It never occurred to me to retrieve any of our things left at the house. I had simply walked away from one dimension of reality into another.

But why didn't I run then? Why hadn't I seen this as the curtain going down over a mad hatter's party? Why had the police seen me as an innocent bystander, and not as one of these druggies?

What struck me most about that moment was seeing Jeff toppled from his drug lord pedestal, and the haunting look of sorrow he gave me. He had been hunted down, caught in the thicket of his folly, and I was left to run for help. This makes no sense except for the boundless ignorance of my soul. I had chosen to bind myself to a man convinced of his own godhood. He held me in sway by an ancient confusion of sex infused with divine power. The joining of our bodies was not merely a chain of chemical reactions, nor the simple exchange of bodily fluids. If we were merely animals instead of Homo sapiens, that would have been all that occurred. However human beings are an organic unity of body, soul, and spirit. I was unable to discern the difference between emotional bondage, forged by drugs powerful enough to drive me deeper into a fantasy world, and the reality of true love.

The next morning I went early to the library and informed my boss that my "husband" would be in that day's newspaper headlines. As a practicing homosexual in the 60s, this professional man had to live life in the shadows of normal society. He said it wouldn't cost me my job, and I was grateful for his kindness. The paper did sport Jeff's picture on the front page, along with salacious descriptions of our party pad activities. The article had exposed me as one of those notorious hippies working in their midst. My secret weekend wild side had been revealed, and I carried my new identity with an uneasy grace. It was a coming out party I hadn't bargained for. I was Jeff's "old lady" to the ones who had escaped the police net and were lying low out of sight, but among the library *intelligentsia*, I was the abused, confused wife of a drug lord. I went on quietly mending old books, typing catalogue cards, and helping readers search for information. Gradually I earned some *tea and sympathy* from some of my colleagues.

A strange new path, carved by untoward circumstances, lay before me, and I ran free, relieved of so much emotional baggage. Jeff was convicted and sent to the medical facility of Vacaville State Prison for two and a half years. To all our amazement they discovered he had TB, which meant I needed to be tested. The results were negative. Both our lives seemed to have been spared from the rapid and destructive downward spiral that almost sucked us into oblivion. His family adopted me out of pity, but I was determined to prove my mettle, and purge my conscience of guilt from the current failure to keep Jeff out of harm's way. Again, I was faced with my own weakness, my own moral paralysis, and it sickened me.

Raymond had remained Kitty's friend despite their divorce. He was a caring, gallant man who had embraced a self-imposed monastic solitude, in which he wrote volumes of poetry. He and Kitty had kicked over all the traces of their Christian heritage when they embraced the workingman's religion called Communism. Their three children suffered being branded as "the kids in red diapers" because their parents had swallowed the ultimate camel, the utopian dream of a classless society. As it turned out, both Raymond and Kitty felt betrayed by the news of Eastern Europe's merciless rape carried out by the Russian Bear. Their own revolution had turned sour, but they still championed the poor, the workingman, and helped establish unions. Kitty was an atheist who remained passionately committed to everyone's right to believe and practice the religious dictates of his conscience. She raised her children according to Freud, Pavlov, Jung, Marx, Maslow, and Mother Nature, not according to Dr. Spock. They were groomed to become self-actualized persons, not shackled by the cultural mores of a pie-in-the-sky Americana. As a consequence, Jeff became a self-serving rebel, who felt more at home among disenfranchised blacks than with his own Anglo-Saxon race. He spoke the black man's jive jargon, drank his cheap wine, learned to play his rhythms on bongos and steel drums, and fully embraced the pot culture that spawned their playful promiscuity.

But behind bars, Jeff became a model prisoner, a gentler soul, more like a gelding than the stud he had been. He wrote poetic letters to me, nurturing a tiny flame of hope that our relationship could be salvaged and healed. I was offered a job again at Kitty's, and worked tirelessly for his mother, learning the fine art of cooking and serving food. My tips enabled me to buy antique furniture from a nearby store: a 1920 Easy copper washing machine, a huge brass bed, and an oak dresser. I was furnishing my future with the odds and ends of a vintage lifestyle that had vanished long ago. Kitty eventually sold the restaurant and bought forty acres in Napa, and I began to fill a small cabin there with my treasures. She would drive me to visit with Jeff every few weeks, and then let us have some private time. He was still wearing the mask of a TB patient, and seemed excited to hear about the property and our new way of life.

Once my mother actually flew from New York to pay us a visit, and came to the prison hospital, excited to meet Jeff. We never talked about the real reason he was there, but only talked about the beauty of our new home, and the future that awaited us. She could see how happy I seemed to be, and stayed with us at Napa for a couple of days. She and Kitty had some tense and interesting political conversations around the kitchen table. Kitty was very respectful of my mother's orthodoxy, and pleasant enough, but I knew my mother suspected that her daughter had joined the red ranks of Marxism. She probably made many a novena for me when she returned home.

Felix and Norma, the previous owners of the property, taught me how to plant a vegetable garden, and it seemed that the simple down-to-earth lifestyle I had craved since childhood was within my grasp. Jeff and I could be safe there, and raise our children in a healthy hard-working atmosphere. We would be far from the *Berzerkeley* crowd and the burnt-out pleasures they pursued. Our life at this point in time seemed to be drug-free, though I later found out Jeff got high in prison regularly. This naive idealistic vision began to fade the day we went to pick up Jeff from prison and bring him home to Napa. I could sense it in his swagger, and the way he grabbed the white shirt I had ironed to honor his day of freedom. He didn't notice that the metal hanger hook had scratched my arm, and a trickle of blood marked the wound.

Our reunion culminated in an impromptu wedding performed by a neighboring minister. We were married in a newly ploughed field, speaking words we had casually written to each other. I really wanted to mean what I said, but there was a gnawing recognition that things would never be as I had dreamed, nor would we ever be closely knit together. I wore a simple blue silk dress I had bought for a quarter at Goodwill, and Jeff wore country overalls. Our witnesses were family and some of Kitty's friends. She seemed delighted with the prospect of seeing her son settle down in such a wholesome setting. I was as nervous as a bride should be, but the reason came from my heart's deeply felt unease. Jeff was going along with the program, so to speak, since he was still on probation. Kitty had bought this property to secure a future home for her children and grandchildren. So, this was a happy day indeed for her. But that dream would die too soon for all of us.

Chapter Six

Bleeding Out in Berkeley

Soon Jeff longed for the old brotherhood of Berkeley and uprooted us again. His mother Kitty had done her best to keep him down on the farm, and onboard with the family program. But back we went into all the familiar places of wildness and weirdness that Berkeley offered. I had kept apart from the drug scene while Jeff was in prison; but he needed to stay high in order to cope with the dullness of normal life, to feed his fantasies and amplify his thrills. He easily lured me back into our old habits of getting high and following the party crowd.

But an event that shaped and shamed our political history tore open our shallow lives momentarily and plunged us into despair. In November of 1963, I remember wearing black and walking barefoot on Telegraph Avenue after we heard the unbelievable news that President John Francis Kennedy had been assassinated. We were convinced that the *system* had taken him out. Shock waves went through every segment of American society. The beatniks and hippies, the young, the restless, and the rebellious were also part of a nation that mourned the man who had stood up to the savage growling of the huge Russian Bear. We all admired Kennedy's classy savoir faire, his idealism and youthful energy, privately smiled at his womanizing, and sensed he had been removed from power because of his potential for greatness as a leader. The deep sense of loss and the endless speculation over the many unanswered questions surrounding his murder only served to confirm for us the fact that our political system was ruled and shaped by power mongers.

Then in early summer, I was delighted to learn I was pregnant again, and this news seemed to briefly propel Jeff into settling down. Raymond had helped us find an apartment in Berkeley, and move some of our furniture there. Then he graciously added me to his medical insurance. Like a good hippie mama, I carried around a small basket of vitamins and herbs instead of a purse. Raymond became a surrogate father, and visited us often with bags of groceries and cash handouts. Making money legitimately hadn't been a part of Jeff's thinking. Only once did he take a job for a week as a waiter at the Caffe Mediterraneum, the iconic coffee house on Telegraph Avenue. But drug buddies soon convinced him that he was a musician and could earn his living playing drums at parties, of which there were plenty. He was handsome and talented enough to cajole women into giving him money in return for his favors. In his eyes, Jeff had paid a pound of flesh for his current freedom, and he would never live behind bars again. The savvy he had gained from two and a half years of prison life had programmed him into a lifestyle of "beating the system."

And so, once again, I had joined Jeff on the painted horses for another merry-go-round party scene, fueled by pot and psychedelics. I still had an occasional toke on a joint, but kept my distance from LSD for a season. The child growing within became a person to me when I suddenly knew her name. The fluttering of little limbs, and the movement of her small body thrilled me. I visually saw an envelope with *Aimée* written in the upper left hand corner, the name of an English teacher who had gently mentored me as a freshman in high school. When someone asked me if I had picked out a name, I quickly said, "Yes, her name is Aimée." It was that clear, and that final. I never once doubted who she was. At the same time, I mourned the death of a marriage that once had seemed like a green flourishing tree, and now was all but withered. I clung to the ripening child within me, and vowed that her life would not be cut short. Withdrawing from the party scene, I entered into a private asylum of my own making, inhabited by some of Jeff's cohorts, a circle of men and women who had stretched their domestic arrangements to the fringes of fantasy and beyond.

There was Pooh, in reality a toothless hooker, though still young and pretty. She was round with child when I first met her, and always laughing. She birthed a beautiful round-eyed boy named Pio, fathered by Ralph, a razor-witted ex-con. He was more friend and protector to her than pimp, and also a self-appointed mentor to all the studs prancing around him. He had promised to buy her a set of teeth, which he finally did, which gave her back some measure of social dignity. Ralph was a short mafia-type Italian, whose charisma, wit, and brilliance was sharpened by the hatred he nurtured against the prison guards, whom he called "pigs." His words had an acerbic edge, and were colored by the raw sewage of prison survival incidents. Pooh seemed titillated by his commentary on the world scene, and his ability to hold center stage. She confided to me that they loved to go to sleazy x-rated movie houses to get turned on. I was only able to return an insipid smile, but inwardly I was repulsed.

Ralph described me as a Botticelli painting, and labeled me a "true believer" in the Norman Mailer tradition. He had sensed I was out of my league. Whenever he took his café table pulpit, all I could see were the jagged lines of pain etched in his face, and I grieved at the depth of his cynicism. He in turn envied and despised my lack of experience, and my innocence only unnerved him. He asked if I had seen Ingmar Bergman's *The Virgin Spring*, which I had, during my class-cutting-for-culture's-sake era in college. Suddenly the image of the young maiden, who had just been savagely raped, bathing in the forest spring, weeping over her lost virginity, came shuddering back into view. He smiled wickedly as he watched the memory pinch my face and cause me to bow my head. Perhaps Jeff had regaled him with the details of my deflowering.

When Ralph began to rack up a considerable number of conquests, Pooh became very friendly to me, and asked what I thought about Jeff's little *amours*. I gave the falsely bravado answer that they were of no consequence to me, as long as they remained a passing fancy. Actually, I was stunned into silence by her blunt question and felt stupid. After all, I reasoned, wasn't the sexual turn-on a rule of the pack? My soul was bleeding out, and my mind was put on hold, locked in a deep freeze, in a mental paralysis of feeling trapped. The festering wounds from our lifestyle had moved my emotions ever-deeper underground.

Pooh's friends, Cookie and Johnny, wandered in and out of our lives. She was a pale-skinned brunette who "turned tricks" for the money to keep her supplied with cocaine and crystal-meth. Her old man was an ex-con like Ralph, who still had enough good looks and devastating charm to prey on the women he called "menopausal commandos." It was all done in fun, wrapped up in generous handouts to buddies, and then turned into dirty jokes around the table. Ralph, Johnny, and Jeff had tapped into a goldmine of "desperate housewives" and divorcees, seeking new thrills. Then, there was Willy, a slick black jive-talking outcast, who had found his healing balm in a sugar-sweet white southern girl named Barbara. She was pregnant with his child, and worked in a restaurant in order to set up a home for them. Willy would ignite himself into tirades of schizophrenic babble against the establishment. Barbara would look on adoringly as we all squirmed and laughed at him. I felt hemmed in by this thick concentric circle of dope smokers, pimps, and madmen, an onlooker who was a prisoner of her own rebellion.

Another friend of quite a different caliber came into that mix. Her name was Ellen, a Jewish folksinger, who was raised bohemian style in Brooklyn, and had traveled to the West Coast to tap into the coffee house scene. My cousin John Francis had met her and introduced us. John had recently left New York and joined me in the Berkeley groove. He was a talented musician, and played drums for burgeoning bands like Country Joe and the Fish and Jefferson Airplane. I had grown up listening to him practice in his family's Bronx basement apartment. He was a favorite cousin who faithfully taught me all the latest Latin dance moves like the mambo, the cha-cha-cha, and the meringue. Growing up, I tagged along with him to dances and enjoyed his popularity, his good looks, hip ways, and musical ability. He had been like a surrogate boyfriend during my teenage years.

Ellen's friendship was a gift from another kind of musical world. She brought to life my old longing to sing, and taught me how to play folk songs on the guitar. Joan Baez and Bob Dylan were our idols then. Whenever I heard Joan's voice, the purity of it made my soul ache, and Dylan's words burned into my heart and mind with the power of prophetic intensity.

Joanie had become the Berkeley students' darling. She had left the Boston coffee house scene to spread her folksy gospel to our generation. I can vividly recall her walking barefoot onto a university stage and mesmerizing us with her simple beauty and thrilling voice. Luckily Ellen's flesh-and-blood New York humor soon cured me of any idolatry. She was confident of our ability to get gigs and make connections. Often we visited KPFA's Midnight Special, a hootenanny style gathering, to share current folk song favorites and listen to new songs. One evening a handsome blond guitarist came in accompanied by a plump, pimple-faced young girl. It seemed an incongruous match until she opened her mouth to sing. Her name was Janice Joplin, and we were privileged to hear her launch her singing career that night. She was a country girl with a mega-voice that rumbled up from deep inside her, and we could only keep silent after she sang. Soon she was swallowed up in Bill Graham's San Francisco Light shows, dance halls, and rock bands. We watched sadly as she gorged herself on drugs and liquor until her life sadly burned out like a shooting star, leaving a tragic trail of sparks as she fell.

I saw her stomp onto Graham's stage one evening, obviously stoned out of her mind, dressed in leathers, looking like a Hells Angels chick who had been in a brawl, and downing a whole quart of Southern Comfort in one smooth gulp to the frenzied screams of her fans. When she opened her mouth to sing, only a hoarse scream emerged to begin her performance. Her voice had cracked and lost its mellow intensity. "Take another piece of my heart now, Baby" was her lament, and the words rang so true. She had been raped into a bisexual lifestyle, and transformed into a foul-mouthed bitch that trumpeted her rage into music. It was truly a shock to see her disintegrate so rapidly before our eyes, as we remembered how she looked, and the power of her voice when she first sang in that homespun jamboree.

Such was the power of the dark side of those days. Souls were sucked into a spiritual vacuum, brains scrambled by psychedelics, bodies whacked by macrobiotics, health diet fads, and sex-trips. Minds were being stripped bare of historical content and culture by Alpert's popular mantra, "Be here now!" Berkeley's halls of learning had been defaced, inscribed with revolutionary graffiti by rebel students. Social values related to normal life were being openly questioned. Suddenly, the playing field had been leveled by young voices challenging the status quo. The new watchwords were: organic, natural, holistic; and the commune was becoming the new ideal lifestyle.

Chapter Seven

A Mutant Queen

Little Aimée grew quietly within me, and gradually became a tiny, invisible guide who gently nudged me to escape this morass in which I was indeed sinking. Jeff took me along at times to Alan Watts' not-so-Zen parties in Sausalito. By the primitive power he displayed when playing steel drums, Jeff had become a celebrity among the *nouveau hip intelligentsia*. Any gathering would soon erupt into a polite but orgiastic dancing frenzy. He introduced me to Alan's daughter, who was forming a La Leche League chapter in San Francisco, and it caused me to think about breastfeeding for the first time. She happily gave me her spiel and seemed awed that I was carrying Jeff's child. Many in that crowd were convinced that Jeff was an Important Person, and wanted to see or do his astrology chart. I suppose that fed his ego and mine momentarily, and blurred the edges of our conjoined insanity, all of which continued to isolate me further from his Telegraph Avenue coterie.

I clung to the name "Mary Stewart" given me by marriage, and hid behind it like a veil of false dignity. People seemed impressed by it and I now had a role to play, that of a mutant queen, or a vagabond's widow. It was a tensile-strength solace at best, and I was not comforted. My soul's moral compass had been tweaked. I was out of kilter, teetering on a knife-edged reality, breathing in more illusion whenever I sucked in the smoke from the joints. I played the silly mind games, gathered know-nothing trivia, learned the art of jive talk, and chased after do-nothing parties. If we choose to create our own destiny with the fabrics handed to us by fate or circumstance, then my world was fragile by anyone's standards.

Ellen found me sad-eyed and dreaming in my apartment. She knew that Jeff was caught up in a new relationship, and wanted to lift me out of my melancholy. I hadn't seen him for quite some time, and the pain of being a castoff was becoming unbearable. "Crazy Jane," my downstairs neighbor, and her beautiful mulatto daughter were my only companions. This little family had adopted me, and I wondered if I would become like them. I silently wondered, "Could they be portents of my future, an early warning system?" Jane's Nordic face was twisted by a painful smile, and her odd jerky gestures made her look even stranger. She spoke the jargon of a spiritualist, which helped explain away her personal tragedies. Her heart was still tender enough to mother me as I faced the beginning of motherhood alone. Her daughter often brought me newly baked cookies and gifted me one day with a delicate white kitten from their brood.

Ellen's own gift to me that day was very different. She was as pregnant as I was, and delighted to be sharing this time with me. I was depressed and without thinking of the consequences, dropped a little acid with her. We played guitar and sang folk songs together, of love born in simple innocence, of love that could leap over death's abyss. She tried to assure me that Jeff really loved me, but my heart was too heavy to make the leap. Just then, my water broke, dispelling the gloom. Ellen rushed downstairs to get Jane, who knew immediately from the smell that I was going into labor. I felt nothing but joy, and wanted to stay there and have my baby in my beautiful brass bed. Jane insisted that I go to the hospital, especially when I told her Aimée was due in February, and this was only December 10.

She helped me to take a shower; Ellen braided my hair, and rode with me in a cab. The walk up those hospital steps was the loneliest of my entire life! I had entered a foreign country. It seemed so strange, so stiff and cold. In every journey toward the unknown, there is a confrontation with loneliness and fear. I walked between two very different worlds in that moment. The nurses and doctor had no idea of the state I was in mentally and emotionally. Suddenly reality ripped through my drugged consciousness. The doctor said brusquely, "Mother, you'd better be praying; your child has only a fifty-fifty chance of making it!" My soul flew immediately to God, and clung to Him, in a rush of fear, shame, and guilt. The nurse gave me a shot to induce labor, since my water had already broken. Within half an hour I was fully dilated and felt the strange urge to push. They wheeled me into the delivery room, where I panicked under the bright lights, terrified by the force of the pains. My ears didn't hear the sounds I was making.

Someone offered me anesthesia to help me relax. Just then the doctor lifted a long slender body from my body. Aimée came out legs first, and with a strong cry! "She's alive and kicking," I thought. The doctor held her up like a glistening doll before me, and said, "Here's your little girl, mother." Grateful tears fell down my face in thankfulness for another mercy I had just received. Next to me a large black woman had just delivered a ten-pound boy, who lay like a trophy on her chest. She looked at me with a grin and a wink. Everything in her world seemed so big and strong. Little Aimée had come triumphantly, but oh, so delicately. She was a preemie, weighing four and a half pounds, and measuring nineteen inches long. The nurse swept her away from me before I had even touched her. I was only allowed to look at her through a thick glass wall, and ached to hold her. Aimée had begun her life in a crisis that I had created. There was no smell of me upon her, no warmth of me to reassure her. This was a self-inflicted agony I had to endure for the next two weeks.

When I confessed my desire to breastfeed, a kind white-haired nurse brought me a breast pump, and taught me how to use it. Mothers were not encouraged to breastfeed during that era, but I remembered my conversation with Alan Watts' daughter telling me about joining the La Leche League. And so I waited in the hospital for three days for my milk to come in. There was no child's cry to release it, and no hungry mouth to receive it. I was determined to purify myself from drugs and alcohol in order to feed her. Her heavenly Father had protected her from my foolishness, and her earthly father was on a sex-trip somewhere. The news that she wouldn't be released until she weighed five pounds sent me into a tailspin. That translated into a two-week wait for her to be all mine. The nurses happily reported to me that Aimée was a like little piglet, gobbling up the formula they gave her, but they never once brought her to me so I could see and touch her. Later I learned that she never needed an incubator, a small miracle and a great mercy.

Jeff finally showed up as I was being released from the hospital. I watched his face as we both peered through the glass wall. He had hoped for a son, and commented only on how little she was. There was more than a glass wall between Jeff and me. His words sounded like jazz riffs coming from a distant room, and he seemed as unreachable as my child.

Was it here that I began to hear the first footfalls of Him who searches for us down the twisted labyrinths of time? The reader must understand that memory can function like a magnifying glass, causing us to look more closely at the spotted, faded photographs of our life, some of which are stuck together, and when separated, nearly obliterate the images. Yet they still have enough residual power to touch the raw nerve endings of ancient wounds, and cause one to draw back in pain.

The next images are fairly clear. Aimée was born on December 10, 1964, and came home two weeks later on Christmas Eve. There were no holiday decorations or joyful carols playing. It must have been Raymond who helped me, who bought the bassinet, and groceries, because Jeff was not in the picture. I remember tenderly laying her down, trembling whenever I touched her. Here was my living doll, my Christmas present from above. She was so exquisitely beautiful, and her skin as transparent as an angel who had come from a higher world. I felt so alone, so guilty, so ignorant of motherhood, and so separated from all that I had gone through before that moment. *How could I bring such a tender and vulnerable child into this primeval party scene of hashish-driven dancing and lunatic-driven drums?*

Suddenly, the person who had been bound and gagged within me stood up, and said, "No! I can't do this anymore." Then I slowly walked into the bedroom, wiping tears as I packed all Jeff's belongings into the suitcase Crazy Jane had given me to go to the hospital. I waited, hovering over Aimée, watching her breathe, so thankful we were together and she was safe. When Jeff finally came home, he sheepishly walked over to us, and mumbled something

I can't remember. I silently pointed him to the bedroom, and the waiting suitcase. If there were any words exchanged, they have disappeared into some well of merciful oblivion. He left almost immediately, and I sobbed at the emptiness of our parting. Aimée's helplessness had given me the courage to say goodbye.

Chapter Eight

Motherhood in Madness

It was time for me to try to feed little Aimée myself. Skin to skin at last, to feel my warmth, learn my smell, and know she had a mother after all. As we rotated her feedings between bottle and breast, she began to grow. I don't know how much milk she got, but I had religiously pumped my breasts prior to her coming home, and had given the milk to my little white kitten. How sad to think of the cultural climate of those days. There was no one to instruct me that I could have frozen the milk and kept it for her. Jeff's sister Leslie came over to watch lovingly as I tried to nurse Aimée. Raymond came as usual with loads of groceries. Abby visited and cheered me up with her smile and sense of humor. They were my only family now, and helped to carry me through sad, lonely hours, surrounding Aimée and me in a loving, caring atmosphere.

We never spoke of Jeff. Kitty reluctantly took on a detached role of grandma, and buried herself in teaching handicapped children and managing her new property in Napa. Abbie's boyfriend Mickey owned some duplexes, and he rented one to us after I became a welfare recipient. Amazingly, I found my friend Ellen living right next door with her "old man" Stan, and their newborn daughter, Frieda. Ellen also had a bright-eyed three-year old boy named Luke from her New York folk singing days. I set to work painting all the walls white, and the wooden floors black! The color scheme made it look more like an art gallery than a home. My antique furniture, artifacts, and rugs helped to transform it into a hippie palace.

Abbie came to live with us then. She stayed in Aimée's room, and loved to play with Aimée as she stood up in her crib, a shining blonde beauty, with rosy cheeks, blue almond eyes, and cherubic mouth. My cousin John Francis, a roving musician, also came to live with us. He claimed the attic as his pad, and escorted many a stoned chick up there on quiet sex-trips, getting them high and listening to music all night. Suddenly our little home had become the happening place. Jeff's friends came now and again to cheer me on, careful not to mention his name. John Francis brought over his musician friends from Country Joe and the Fish, a rising star rock band in which he played drums. He had successfully arrived on the Berkeley music scene, and shared his hour of glory with me.

I began to enjoy life again, though a modicum of self-flagellation was embedded in my psyche as I followed George Ohsawa's macrobiotic diet to the "jot and tittle," and reduced my weight to 93 pounds. Years later, when I saw a photograph of me sitting on the porch of that house, it was a reminder of how desperate I was then to separate flesh from spirit. Ohsawa had promised his disciples a purified, disease-free body if we stopped eating meat, chewed raw brown rice two hundred times, and ate slowly sautéed carrots with homemade sesame salt. (*It was reported in the news years later that he died of a heart attack brought on by salt shock, though he had really been consuming too much beer or a favorite homemade soda resembling Coca-Cola.*)

Aimée had plump rosy cheeks because she ate baby food, yogurt, avocado, and bananas. She had blossomed into a gorgeous cherub and outgrown her earlier colicky days and nights of crying. Of course I was convinced that her pain was my fault. Sometimes the sound of her constant crying would so upset me that I had to leave the room so as not to vent my anger and frustration on her. By her first birthday she had reached her normal weight, and we celebrated it in typical *bourgeois* style. I made a banana cake topped with whipped cream, strawberries, and a number 1 candle. She sat in her wooden high chair, surrounded by an "admiring bog": some of Jeff's friends and my neighbor Ellen's family, who were all mostly stoned. We sang "Happy Birthday" as I blew out her candle. Her eyes sparkled like sapphires as I handed her a piece of cake. She poked at it, and then buried her face in the whipped cream. We all laughed with delight, but I felt somewhat envious of her freedom.

My life was being redeemed through hers, and I reveled in each step she took, each syllable she uttered. The first year of a child's life is so filled with wonders of discovery and miracles of communication. For some reason she called water "lulu," and when she first saw the ocean she pointed with delight, jumping up and down, calling it "big lulu." Her little life built a bridge of hope between our hearts, and I was beginning to heal. Ellen and I had fun dressing up our doll babies, and gussying-up their second-hand strollers. I painted the ugly aluminum a golden bronze, sewed velvet material on the seat cover, and glued colorful strips of velvet ribbons over the handlebars, adding a bike bell as the final touch. We were quite the "drama mamas" going to the grocery stores and the laundromat, and enjoyed turning heads as we went. The world seemed beautiful for the moment, and Aimée was so much more than a flower child's daughter. For me, and so many others, she became a golden-haired princess that should be displayed and admired on this homemade hippie-style throne on wheels.

Then a chilling wind stirred the Berkeley grapevine, and I began to hear people whispering Jeff's name. He was back in town, they said. *Can you imagine that my heart leapt like a schoolgirl's?* I was indeed a captured bird, chained to a perch, after enjoying a brief flight in the sun. Jeff may only have been curious to see such a gorgeous replica of his flesh, or he may have planned to test the waters with me. The memory of his visit was more like a haunting. He suddenly appeared at the house and people scattered away in every direction. He came and watched me change Aimée's diaper and put her to bed, then shared my bed for one evening before he vanished again like the phantom husband he was. His friends may have been hoping for a reunion of sorts. They didn't understand that there was no place for Jeff with us. Our lives together had reached an impasse. He had forfeited his role as a father and husband in exchange for the freedom to exploit his sexuality to the fullest. It must have been strange for us both to learn that in touching me he couldn't really touch me. I was safely locked behind my heart's door, and that was the last time we ever came together as man and wife.

It is difficult to describe the mystical tension that holds body and soul together. The emotional pain of betrayal and abandonment had nearly severed the silver cord, and the golden bowl was in a meltdown. The desperate path I had carved out of this chaos was a religious potpourri of Buddhist and Hindu philosophy: the material world was an illusion; the spiritual world was true reality, which one experienced as light and energy. My present life was a karmic dilemma, and my attitude swung between acceptance and renunciation of any attachment to it.

Hallucinogenics have a way of making sense of the absurdities, and smoking marijuana reinforces the need for escape routes from the daily grind. Add the Beatles' music as background filler and you have the making of a film noire. Furthermore, add Albert Camus' take on life as a room with "no exit," and there you have the existential version of hell. There are no flames there, but the landscape smolders with an atmosphere of hopelessness. Aimée and I would walk through these ashen fields aimlessly, because I was literally without a clue.

She was my dear companion for the next five years, and like a tender green shoot of hope, the only visible sign of life I saw. Days and months were buried in unconscious subsistence rituals. Berkeley was still the backdrop for us, but became only a blur of touchstone memories. Aimée remained a focal point for any further movement in life.

After I had gotten a new job in a bookstore, we moved to another small house. John Francis continued to live with us. Abby literally flew in and out of our lives as she developed her career as an airline stewardess, loving a life of not settling down for even one second. She would later surprise us all by going back to school and studying to become a nurse. This next job had come through an amazing set of circumstances involved with friendships I had formed at the library.

Alcides and Katherine, an unusual Catholic couple played a very important role in anchoring me to everyday life back in those days. He was a dashing Panamanian student at UCB, and she was a tall Irish lass who spoke perfect French and Spanish. His Latin *anima* combined with her genteel propriety made for a fascinating marital persona. At first they had provided me with a job of babysitting their three-year-old named Jaime, or Jimmy, while I was waiting for Jeff to be released from prison. Somehow they had more than enough compassion to reach out again during my latest round of failure. I remember being in awe as I watched Katherine morph into a fiery Latina when she disagreed with Alcides, and back again into a docile Irish mother quietly taking charge of their lives.

Katherine had become good friends with an expert book mender in the library who taught us all how to make a simple paste from flour and water to use in repairing old books. Katherine's friend and her husband had just bought one of the many antiquated bookstores, so ubiquitous in Berkeley, and had convinced her to join them in their venture. Work was a necessity for Katherine in order to support her husband's pursuit of a Master's degree in Political Science, and ultimately as an important official employed by his government. The bookstore also needed a part-time helper, and she had suggested me for the job. That meant I had to leave Aimée, now two years old, in my cousin's care. It wasn't an easy decision, but he had mornings free and seemed to enjoy the company of children.

My strange looks and manner intrigued the husband, a bearded intellectual, but disturbed his wife. When I overheard her telling Katherine that she thought I was a child of the devil, I was shaken. Her phrase made me wonder what I had become, and how others really viewed me. A few more uncomfortable weeks went by until I got an urgent phone call from my cousin telling me Aimée had fallen down and hit her head. She had gone into convulsions and he had called an ambulance after trying to help her. At least he had the presence of mind to call 911, but was so freaked out by what had happened that he couldn't explain to me over the phone why or how she had fallen. He was never able to coherently tell me the real story.

I took a cab and rushed to the hospital, and almost fainted when I saw her lying in a tub of ice, shivering violently, a thermometer clenched in her mouth. Her eyes were so glazed with fever that she didn't recognize me. The nurses warned me not to become hysterical, or I couldn't stay there. So, I shook with silent sobs, and was sure this was somehow my fault. Aimée's temperature had climbed well beyond 104 degrees and she was in dangerous waters. I must have prayed in some mysterious way as I helplessly watched them bring her out of the death zone. Then she was whisked to a room, and I had to consent to them giving her a spinal tap. The doctors were sure she had spinal meningitis, and I listened to her screams from the corridor, crunched up in a chair as I felt her pain. They decided to keep her a week for more observation. I visited her often, and she jumped with joy in her crib when she saw me, not understanding why she was there. Thankfully, she was released to me because the doctors couldn't find any cause for her convulsions.

This mysterious event evoked renewed sympathies in Kitty, and at her invitation I quit my job, and moved to Napa where she lived part time. Now Aimée and I walked over country roads, and stayed in the small house that the previous owners had built, and now Kitty's country home. This was a better place to shield Aimée from harm, and where she had been conceived. Raymond came to visit us, and stayed in the cabin where Jeff and I had lived. I called Aimée *petite chou*, a French pet name meaning, "little cabbage head." It was an endearment used commonly in France, and it slowly evolved into both of us calling her *chouchou*. He inadvertently spelled it, "shoo-shoo." We both spent time playing with Aimée, and delighted in her drawings, and precocious language ability. Kitty played the role of an interested but distant grandmother. She had decided to trade part of her Napa equity to purchase a dance hall and bar called The New Orleans Club in Berkeley. It was her way of buying into the counter-culture that Jeff and I had adopted. She was excited and proud to take Aimée and me there, wanting to see our reaction. Its size and potential were impressive, and we laughed as Aimée ran around the huge dance floor between the chairs and tables, enjoying all the empty space. Kitty could be both eager entrepreneur and energetic swinger. She had mastered the politics of neutrality, as Jeff was never part of our conversation. Of course, he did stop by to check it all out, obviously proud of his "hip" mother. Aimée and I were shuttled back and forth between Napa and Berkeley, helping Kitty establish her new business. It brought back the missing elements of entertainment and excitement to our quiet country existence.

Kitty never introduced me as her daughter-in-law, but proudly showed off her gorgeous granddaughter to all the customers. She wanted to free me from any *bourgeois* constraint, and subtly encouraged me to form new relationships with the New Age band rockers who came to play, especially a tall blonde violinist who was attracted to me. But I couldn't step beyond the friendly conversation barrier. After all, she and Raymond were "friends" despite her other marriages and series of amours. Raymond had resigned himself to live at a detached distance while remaining the consummate dad, and now the devoted grandpa. They were prepared to support Jeff and me going through the same cycles. We were held together by a legally binding piece of paper, and I didn't have the courage to render it powerless. The iconic name of Mary Stewart was the only means I had of keeping a shred of self-worth.

Chapter Nine

Endgame

Life came then in the form of husks and crumbs, and I chewed on whatever came my way. I was, in a sense, at Kitty's mercy, and clung to the family circle she had provided. Who knows what her own dreams had demanded of her, or why she was driven to build an all-inclusive estate that would encompass her very independent family? The power to do this was in her hands, and in her heart. This place would make room for us all if we would agree to recognize her sovereignty. *And who knows how many times her dreams had been dashed to pieces, and her heart crushed, as mine had been? And in the end, could she have foreseen that her house would be divided against itself?*

The forty acres she had purchased was indeed a decent spread, and it needed a goodly number of hands to keep it going. Like a formidable sovereign, she courted people who would contribute to her kingdom. And many of her loyal friends did. Notably, a whole family had come to help: Tom, an artistic flamboyant carpenter, who shared Kitty's penchant for drinking bouts; Jody, his wife and companion, who relished their shared life, a series of nomadic soul-searching impromptu adventures; and their delightful children (who skip by namelessly in memory). Tom's vision was to flesh out the rotting skeleton of a stagecoach building, once a stopping-off place for travelers, the only remnant of the property's past history. He wanted to fill it with antiques, like the ones I had gathered but had left behind in Berkeley. The only piece of mine that remained was an old copper washing machine. Kitty especially liked his proposal of a zero money exchange. She would provide materials, room, and board. It seemed like an ideal arrangement. Kitty had her property management team in place, and things could progress rapidly. This family had been witness to my marriage to Jeff, and our subsequent return to Berkeley.

Their wedding gift had been a magnificent hand-pieced Victorian quilt that graced our antique brass bed. Tom had presented it with much ceremonial pomp, but his wife's obvious chagrin over losing their family treasure choked much of the moment's joy away. I was embarrassed by his surprising magnanimous gesture and tried to protest for Jody's sake. Somehow in all my wanderings, I managed to hang on to it for many years, because I valued the sacrifice it had represented, and the amazing handwork it displayed. However, trouble was brewing in Yuba City. Tom had meandered down the road to visit a lovely neighbor's wife who had caught his eye and his soul. Jody gritted her teeth against the untimely appearance of this intruder she nicknamed the Queen of Sheba, and endured the tensions of a love triangle for a season. Tom confessed to me that he had been intrigued by her neurotic insecurities, and offered to become her Zen master and lover in order to free her. The end of the affair was finally sealed when Jody happily announced she was pregnant.

They soon drifted on to fairer pastures and now Leslie was happily in love with another young man, also named Tom, who came to live on the property. He too was an architect with a vision. They carried on the work that the other Tom had begun, and were now running Kitty's affairs on the property. Soon they built their own house in the meadow where Jeff and I had been married. After Leslie and Tom had a daughter she decided to earn her own degree in architecture from a college in Napa. It was Leslie who told me that Jeff and family were coming for a visit on their way back to Big Sur. Kitty was not about to give her estranged son a welcome mat. because he had chosen the Big Sur lifestyle, effectively severing his ties to the ranch. But my own life's dilemma was being framed in a time-lapse photograph, like the slow moving dance of a whirling dervish, taunting me to escape from being marooned on this island.

Surely the dreaded "leftover life" that I had feared after leaving New York had become my current reality.

Jeff drove up the gravel road, in colorful caravan style. He had brought along his wacky friend Ron, his friend's wife Storm, and their firstborn son, River. I don't remember others in the picture, or even seeing Carol, his "old lady," and their new baby daughter. Surreal can't begin to describe the emotional landscape of that visit. Strange new figures moved in freestyle caricatures of themselves around me, and I floated between them, hardly able to speak a word of sense. Jeff let me know that this was his family now, and I was welcome to join it, and they would be leaving the next day.

How strange was this? Here was a woman who had been with Jeff when Aimée was born and I was left alone. The thought of causing her some anxiety was delicious, though I had no intention of flirting with Jeff. Why would I leave the security of the ranch to throw my lot in with these Big Sur Crazies?

Reason had no part in my decision to join them. I was bored with the predictable, the expected, and the joyless sentence of life imprisonment in a safe place, under the guise of faithfulness to an illusory marriage relationship. Something vital had been taken from me, that much I could fathom. But how to redeem myself, and reclaim a life from these ruins seemed out of reach for me then. The only option left for me was this desperate attempt to find separateness, and an endgame move to change the dynamics of an otherwise stultified life.

Kitty may have been shocked at my impropriety or what she deemed my stupidity. She certainly felt betrayed by my decision. After all she had been our caretaker since Jeff and I had parted. I may also have disappointed Leslie by what seemed a groveling gesture on my part. Perhaps she was hoping I could find the strength to face life without him and find someone new. Jeff seemed delighted at the result of his new power play.

And so I followed him once again, this time on an emotional odyssey to Big Sur, once the choice haven of dissident artists and writers. Now it was slowly becoming the psychedelic playground of the rich and famous, the yellow submarine for dopers and dropouts, a sacred cow for spiritualists and a garden of paradise for naturalists. Big Sur had expanded its borders yet again to embrace the tensions of such a diverse society, which in turn would only enrich its social image of tolerance, while adding yet another dimension to its all-inclusive culture.

As Bob Dylan's song goes, "The times they are a changing." Now it was my time to exchange a lonely habitat for this mysterious land etched with such dramatic beauty, filled with enchantments and dreams. The vision of its power to free me from the misery of past failures was like a beacon of light drawing me into its harbor. I was taking a bold step toward liberation from all that was false and unnatural . . . or so I thought. If only I could have foreseen then that a much heavier, darker bondage awaited me.

Photo Memorabilia

Mother and Dad's Wedding Day

Our family in the Quonset Hut

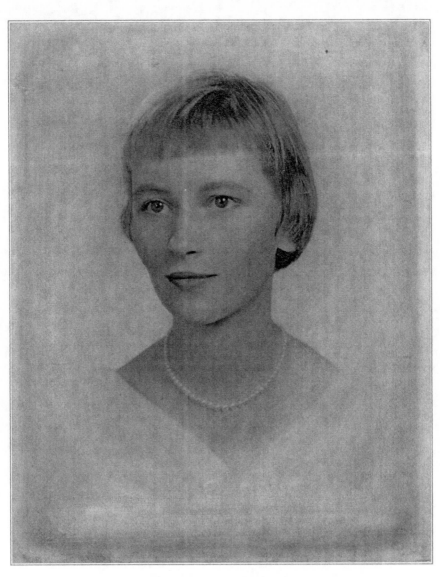

High school Graduate

Mary and Lucy on the Ridge

Aimée in Vogue Magazine

Mary and Aimée at Nepenthe

Lucy and Aimée

Lucy, age 3

Aimée at School

Big Sur Fellowship

PART THREE: BIG SUR
Land of My Second Birth

"Make haste my beloved and be like a gazelle or
a young stag on the mountain of spices."
(Song of Songs 8:14, NKJV)

Chapter One

"Les Enfants du Paradis"

Little Aimée and I, with a large wooden box that could easily pass for a coffin and that contained all our earthly possessions, were on the road again. We had just spent several months at a commune called Point 16 located directly opposite a painted white cross that marked the location of the Camaldoli Hermitage, an order of monks committed to silence and prayer, who lived on top of the mountain. Years later I visited them with a friend, and my Irish Catholic mother. They were selling their world-famous brandy-laced fruit cakes, and offering retreats for a new generation of spiritual burnouts.

Were they praying for us then, down below, the dope-smoking hippies, heroin addicts, cocaine shooters, and drifters? And for me, a lost hippie mama and her beautiful child, a child ignored by her own father, and fawned over by everyone else?

Though Carol, Jeff's current "old lady" had given him another girl, he seemed only interested in generating progeny and giving others the gift of raising them. He told me once that he would have many children and believed his gene pool was worth spreading around. I didn't want to believe him then, early on in our marriage, but that has turned out to be his legacy. Consequently, I had jumped into an emotional cauldron of my own making. It was I who had deliberately stepped into Jeff's new family circle. Why do something so blatant? "The heart has reasons Reason knows not of." I was compelled to try another lifestyle; one so different from anything I had known before. I felt more like a runaway bride who refused to be under her mother-in-law's thumb forever.

Did I yet nourish any hope for a restored marriage, even the shared kind? Because my mind was so unhinged, I probably did. We were still legally married, but had not been intimate for a couple of years. And there was certainly a twinge of wanting to stick it to Carol a little for the pain she had caused me two years earlier when she wooed Jeff away. Only twisted motives can lie inside a darkened mind and a broken heart. One thing seemed clear in this mixture: I was escaping from the expectations of ordinary society, to become an initiate into an artistic, party going, sex-tripping, break-free commune.

Many neighbors visited the commune and were curious about Aimée and me, and why we had come. We may have added some spice to the local color, some of whom were the notorious South Coasters, devotees of the drug culture who had forged a reputation for hosting wild, full-moon dancing orgies. Others were painters and sculptors whose families were living out Rousseau's dream, and had made a niche in Big Sur society. Most of them were spiritual seekers of an uncommon sort.

That's when I first met Roland Hall and his gorgeous wife Irene. He looked every whit the bearded artistic holy man, and spoke with a gentle mesmerizing voice. As they were leaving our compound, Irene sauntered behind him in red high heels, wearing a long jeans skirt, slit high enough to show her shapely legs. Bill Wiesjahn, the head honcho, whispered to me in a kind of awe, that she was his former wife and the mother of his beautiful blonde children. Bill was a jazz pianist who liked chasing the riffs that heroin gave him. Irene seemed to be the epitome of a Big Sur queen who was strong enough to follow her heart's desire. She must have become tired of raising her children alongside Wiesjahn's menagerie of musicians.

As a South Coaster now, I was taught that our lifestyle could be informed by consulting an oracle, the *I Ching* or *Book of Changes*. The practice promised to guide us in a path always in flux between the dualities in nature that Taoism calls yin and yang. It involved a ritual throwing of three ancient Chinese coins, and a divining of hexagrams that led to a series of pithy epitaphs of wisdom. It became another kind of mystical crapshoot, whose answers never seemed to stick. I was desperately grasping at any spiritual straws thrown my way.

Jeff and his musical band of brothers, and some female followers that danced whenever he and Ron played drums, had managed to become the new main attraction at Wiesjahn's scene. Storm, a lovely, gracious woman, elegant as a French Renaissance painting, was one of the dancers. Her face was softly rounded, framed by luxuriant long hair that she mostly twisted up in a knot, and her pink mouth was perfectly shaped in a cupid's bow. Her name seemed antithetical to her nature. She was more like a graceful cascading fountain, and once shared with me that dancing was her "cup of life." I had never met anyone as uniquely authentic as she was. She and Ron, Jeff's compadre, had a cute little boy named River. Watching her chase down this shirt-topped toddler's naked bottom, frantically trying to wipe up his droplets from Wiesjahn's newly hand-waxed oak floor, was so charming, that even he uttered, "You're a gas, Storm!" I later heard that she and Ron had named their next son Ocean, continuing on in their mother's tradition.

She and Carol made for all the ladies a communal uniform they called "harem pants." Using an old treadle machine, they sewed Indian bedspread material into flowing pants to be worn just above the navel, with a matching top. I was skinny and reveled in my flat belly while Carol's was still plump from childbirth. I enjoyed the looks of Jeff's male friends but ignored the overtures from Bill. It was he who had consented to Jeff and friends moving onto the property. I was not about to become a member of his harem, or anyone's squaw in this tribe. But there we were, a woman and child who seemed to belong to no one, yet treated very kindly. I learned to cook rice on an open fire, make yogurt, plant a garden, and was generally thrilled to learn the health-loving, nature-wise ways of Big Sur folk.

This was the simplicity of life I had longed for since childhood, when I first experienced the great outdoors at summer camps. That was a season filled with memories of nature hikes, learning to fish from a canoe, and skinny-dipping in moonlit lakes. Being raised in the New York slums caused me to thirst for the beauty of unspoiled nature. It was a rare treat to walk in Central Park, visit the zoo, and ice-skate at Rockefeller Plaza. Taking the subway to Coney Island beach, swimming in chlorine-soaked city pools, and opening fire hydrants were the traditional summer refreshment. Occasional trees stuck in concrete sparsely shaded us, and were targeted by every dog in the neighborhood. Life in New York had been like living in a desert, sprinkled with an occasional oasis.

Ed Culver the mailman was also an important part of the Big Sur scene. He drove his van down daily during the week with the mail, sundries (including diapers), and lots of ready-to-eat food, and he allowed us to keep a tab until we could pay him. But I don't think he really kept tabs on any of us. He was a gift for so many who depended on him for sustenance, and became a folk hero down through the years. I bought fruit, milk, and ice cream regularly as there was no refrigeration. Our home was a plastic greenhouse where Aimée and I slept together on a wooden slatted platform.

Our tribe descended on Esalen Institute often to play music and dance for the tourists. I loved being immersed in the hot sulfur baths, perched on the edge of cliffs overlooking the ocean. It was a gorgeously raw sensual experience. There I learned the art of being naked without shame. Ah, this was the new Eden, and we were the stardust children who had reclaimed our lost Paradise. We were all politely pretending not to notice our bodies, and the sexuality they radiated, but insisted on our right to remain innocent as children. Ravi Shankar once gave a concert there, and his music provided the perfect background for our fantasy world. He loved the fact that children were running around, some naked, some colorfully dressed, and all as free as the birds. We sat stoned on the thick African kikuyu carpet of sun-warmed grass, still as young eager yogis, spellbound by the unending ragas. LSD and marijuana kept our group coming back to this mystical playground, again and again, as if to claim it for our earthly inheritance.

Esalen Institute, named after the tribe of Indians who first discovered the baths, had an immense organic garden from which delicious health food was prepared, and visitors from all over the world were coming to partake of the mystique, and endure the rigors of their new experimental techniques, like "Primal Therapy," utilizing the idea of a primal scream, and "Rolfing," a painfully deep tissue massage. My own personal experience of being "Rolfed" proved to be very powerful. Hidden recesses of my soul were opened up as the young girl masseuse plied the tense muscles of my body. I began to quietly sob, weeping for the first time in many years, letting go of the trapped pain. She quietly left the room out of respect for what I needed to release. It was a time of psychological exploration, of going to the extremely fragile edges of sanity, and of exchanging radical ideas and theories. I once overheard someone whispering about a man who hung himself after a brutal group-probing of his psyche. I remember seeing an open toilet on the lawn, which children were being taught to use in order to overcome any privacy hang-ups.

It may seem even stranger yet, but I actually hung around until I witnessed an affectionate reunion between Jeff and Carol. As long as I hadn't seen them together, I could handle the situation. He had been away for awhile earning money by dealing drugs in San Francisco, and had brought her a gift. Out of a paper bag, he pulled out a funky fur coat that he had gotten from a Goodwill store, and gallantly put it on her. Storm saw the pain in my eyes, and took me outside just in time to watch an immense shower of shooting stars. Tears melted them together against the black sky. The deeply buried hope of being his favorite wife evaporated into the immensity of that moonless night. The next day I finally had the courage to corner Jeff alone. He was playing the bongos when I asked him "Who is your wife?" He said, without looking at me, "I have no wife." My response was, "You have said it," and I felt released from the bondage of this relationship.

Then I found Aimée and told her we were leaving. We said an awkward goodbye to the group who had cared for us, but who must have been relieved that I finally "got" it. We went through the gate, crossed the road to the other side (which headed north) and waited for a ride, standing near the bone-white Camaldoli cross. One of the locals recognized us, and wanted to know where we were going. He was kind enough not to ask too many questions. I had no idea where to go, or what to do, and asked him for a suggestion. "Nepenthe is a cool place," he said grinning, "and Lolly, the owner, has helped a lot of people." As we climbed gratefully into the back of his truck, our direction and destiny had once again changed. We had found no place for us in this portion of Paradise.

Aimee on Neptenthe Terrace

Chapter Two

In the house of No Sorrow

A steep climb up a stony path led into the land of Nepenthe, and what seemed to be a mountaintop from which to view our new homeland. This was unexpected higher ground. The angel sculpture that guarded the entrance to the red terrace had a dark, ominous beauty, like a blackened tree trunk rescued from a raging fire. Buzz Brown, a local sculptor, had unearthed a huge piece of fallen redwood while digging around his cabin and carved this unearthly presence that greeted us. He said it represented the Egyptian angel of death who escorted souls across the river Styx to their eternal rest.

Nepenthe soon began to cast its spell. It became a huge window of light that stretched as far south as the eye could follow, and spread my soul wide open. Below the red terrace was the shimmering silver ocean colored by an intensely blue sky. Brown-skinned cattle stood motionless eating away the avalanche of grass on the steep green hills around us. I breathed in the salted, windswept perfume of this fabled "House of No Sorrow." Some six years earlier, I had watched a couple fly across this same dance floor with such abandonment. It was my first encounter with a folk goddess, an older woman named Carol, who wore a long flowing skirt and sandals, elegantly dancing in the moonlight. I trembled then at her shameless display of female power. Her escort was a local artist named Peter. Ironically, Jeff had first introduced us to Nepenthe and the beauty of Big Sur. Now he and I were living here, light years apart. He had secured his position in paradise, and I was still searching for a way in.

The next steps I took were awkward. Perhaps it was Holly, one of Bill and Lolly Fassett's daughters, who first saw us. She may have known why we had come. Big Sur doesn't hold many secrets for long. Then I remember being ushered into the living room and before a queenly presence. Aimée and I sat on her mother's broad chenille-covered couch in the log cabin home as I told our story. Her lovely round face shone, and a deeply dimpled smile radiated warmth and magnetism. She nodded with quiet understanding. Lolly was a tall, buxom woman, of regal posture, dressed in a colorful oriental tunic and slacks. This was her preferred costume in those days. She sat on a divan against the back wall, legs drawn up comfortably, and was busy at some handwork. When I asked her if we could stay, both my distress and Aimée's angelic face must have touched her mother's heart. All she had to offer us was a corner in her sewing room, she said. But it was a place to begin again. I felt so grateful, and offered to work, to clean, to sew, to do anything in order to pay for our keep.

The room had benches with pillows along the wall, which we could use for a bed. Bolts of colorful fabric, thread, and sewing machines were spread across wooden tables. The damp redwood had a comforting smell as we made a place to call our own. Soon we were sitting in Lolly's famous family kitchen talking with Faye, the cook. She assured us we would be fed and housed, and that we were safe. After our first meal at the huge table, I helped wash dishes. I shared about my cooking experience at Jeff's family restaurant and offered to help her in the kitchen. Aimée had found some children outside and was soon playing on the terrace. It seemed to be a painless transition from one lifetime to another.

My soul was fragmented by the search for wholeness and meaning, and my mind still ripped open to nonstop intense sensory perceptions by drugs. The potent cocktail of LSD, peyote, cheap wine, and pot had derailed me from enjoying the common stuff of life. The lines had been blurred. Like the captives in Plato's cave, I had been mesmerized by mere shadows on the wall, and had failed Basic Life Course 101 thus far. Still, I knew I needed help. Aimée was a little over three years old then, full of innocent curiosity and energy, so trusting and forgiving, even though I treated her more like my little sidekick, instead of a child with a confident parent who knew where she was going.

Aimée and I spent many hours there in Lolly's living room, chatting, crocheting, and knitting along with her, and looking at her treasured collection of Little Golden Books. She made sure I watched the historic landing on the moon, and I was thrilled to be part of her family, just one of the many foundlings who had learned to knit and crochet there. I remember knitting Aimée a colorful jumper using round needles. Her delicate blond beauty was once photographed for Vogue magazine while wearing it. Encouraged by Lolly to try different techniques, I knit a huge cape out of aqua and green rug yarn using her huge wooden needles. Under her tutelage it became a work of art, and I sold it for two hundred dollars to pay for my Rolfing therapy at Esalen, joining the circle of Big Sur artisans. The cabin's atmosphere was charged with the creative energy of this family. Lolly delighted in complimenting the slightest bud of talent in anyone. Bright paintings festooned the rough log walls, books spilled out of nooks everywhere, and richly colored fabrics and skeins of wool cascaded out of baskets. There was always a rich feast for the senses.

I knew little then about the Fassett family's artistic history, but relished learning about life in Big Sur whenever Lolly shared her stories. She spoke in awe of her son Kaffe who had achieved international recognition for knitting fabulous sweaters. The local heroes were spawned from families who had pioneered the rugged mountains and coastlands, and artists who had found their inspiration and freedom there. A constant stream of colorful legends walked through the open door of that living room, local residents who helped create the larger than life landscape at Nepenthe: Amelia Newell, whose long white hair flowed over medieval looking robes; Doug Madsen, a marvelous dancer and showman who rode a magnificent white stallion onto the terrace one evening; Peter Monk, a rotund British pundit; Helen Morgenrath and Sylvia Rudolph who waited tables with such elegance and aplomb; Chaco, a Russian jack of all trades; petite Willie Nelson, the daughter of the George Lopes family, part chef and part comedienne, and a dark-haired beauty called Mary Belle, a single mom who served as Nepenthe's manager.

The gaps in my memory grow ever widening from here. Pain has pushed so much of the past into a crevice beyond my reach. I know I worked at the River Inn down the road as a cocktail waitress for a short while. A woman named Diane had come into our lives with an opportunity to earn money and share a cabin with her here. I wore my harem pants and handkerchief top, and played the Big Sur native well . . . that is until some drunken customer decided to pull on the elastic waist to see if I was wearing underwear. Diane stayed on but I quit. Serving drinks to tourists and being pawed by them was not my kind of scene.

Diane was hard to fathom. She was an older, dainty platinum blond who trembled a little, perhaps from taking too much acid. Once she thought we could push her VW bug that had run out of gas up an incline. This was an insane moment I would have nightmares about for many years. Of course we were not strong enough, and the car began to roll backwards. We had to let go, and as it passed us, I saw little Aimée staring out the back window terrified. I screamed and ran down after her, watching the car stop and roll over onto its roof, lying in a small creek bed. We helped Aimée, who was about five years old then, climb out. Luckily it had gone only a short distance. Shaken to the core, I hugged her hard against me, tearful and thankful for the mercy that spared her life from my foolishness.

Diane and I proved to be not a good combination. She easily brushed the incident off as karmic luck, but I was horrified at being so stupid. She and her younger, very handsome boyfriend were convinced they were meant to be lovers, having mapped out their lives using astrology. She went on to have his child, and after laboring for too many hours at home, came close to losing her life while giving birth to their son. Some friends sensed she was really in danger and rushed her to the hospital in Monterey just in time. I don't remember seeing her much after that, but heard that she and Kevin eventually parted ways.

The next episode that comes into view in my memory is when Don McQueen and his wife offered to let us stay in a small trailer near their home in the Big Sur Campground. I was cleaning cabins in two campgrounds to earn a living. Barbara became very fond of us, and wanted to help. She was appalled that I didn't want Aimée learning how to read yet. My reasons were merely reactionary against anything that followed normal educational trends. I explained that I didn't want anything artificial to shape her experience with nature. Of course it made no sense. The truth was that my tormented mind couldn't rest long enough to nurture Aimée's childhood. Since I had to work every day, Barbara offered to care for her. Of course she read many books to her, and Aimée was soon reading on her own. Secretly, I was glad she could play with their children, Jonathan and Torre, and could enjoy being part of a family situation. This only underscored my self-assessment: I was an unfit mother.

That I truly was unfit was proven out in a dramatic and painful lesson. I still had a habit of smoking, and fell asleep with a lit cigarette. Aimée was lying on a floor mat in the front of the trailer. It must have been an angel who awakened me before the lethal fumes could have rendered us both unconscious. I stumbled outside with the mattress, puking, coughing, and yelling for Aimée to get out. Luckily she had been sleeping just under the layer of smoke, and didn't seem affected, another stroke of mercy. Don had heard the commotion and came outside to see what had happened. I was so embarrassed, and promised I would never smoke in bed again, a promise I kept. Don knew how guilty I felt and whistled out "That was a close call!" He just doused the mattress with water and threw it away, and must have let us sleep in his home that night.

This was also the time we met Mae Brussell, and her family. They came regularly to the campground for the summers, and she and her daughters befriended us. They loved Aimée, and gathered us under their wings for a season. Much later I learned that Mae was a revered figure, called by some the Queen of Conspiracy in local politics, and had a radio show called "World Watch." A brilliantly persuasive speaker, she came armed with all the facts she had garnered from cross-referencing the evidence listed in the entire 26 volumes of the Warren Commission Hearings. Mae was convinced that the CIA was behind Kennedy's assassination, that ex-Nazis had infiltrated our government, and that she and her family were on their watch list. She was then grieving the loss of her teen-age daughter Bonnie through a bizarre auto accident, which she attributed to foul play, and had reported receiving many death threats, some from the Manson family. She told me of her earlier love affair with Big Sur and Henry Miller with great gusto. He had liberated her from all her Jewish middle-class hang-ups, so she really identified with the hippie counterculture and its struggle for independence from what we considered to be fascist governmental mind control. We continued to stay in contact with her family for many years until Mae was struck down by cancer, and died peacefully in a Carmel hospice.

Don's campground manager began making overtures to me. He viewed me as a "make love, not war" type of hippie, subtly offering to set me up in his very nice home, and take care of Aimée and me, in exchange for my favors. Mae thought it sounded like a good situation for us. I reminded him of someone with whom he had a pot-fumed love affair, or so he said. But I was not about to become anyone's playmate, and that put pressure on me to find another place to live. That's when I was offered a job working in the Phoenix gift shop at Nepenthe, and when a beautiful woman named Elizabeth offered to share her lovely home with us. She was gracious and cultured, and engaged in an affair with an older gentleman who shared her passion for health foods. She loved cooking and tried to help me make a piecrust once. It was so beyond my ken at that point that I threw the sticky glob from the counter into the sink, shocking us both into laughter and tears.

The time frame of how long we stayed with her is lost. I do remember walking through the dark woods to her place without a flashlight one night, and Aimée holding my hand because I was woozy from wine. Because of our lifestyle, Aimée had developed a steady maturity that guarded a very sensitive heart. Children have such amazing loyalty, and an ability to forgive their parents, despite our neglect. I was blinded by failure and betrayal, yet she continued to see past my pain and senseless meanderings. She was a cast-off jewel entrusted to me, and I was a lonely woman lighting matches in the dark, to keep us both in the land of the living.

As is typical of many New Yorkers, I had never learned to drive. Traveling in Big Sur and beyond was strictly on foot in those days, and by thumb. An important part of the culture was to be identified as a member of the tribe, the bohemian brotherhood. Aimée and I were familiar figures on the coastal road by now and were always given a lift. When I traveled back to Big Sur from town, my instincts taught me to turn down any offer that came from a suspicious looking square. So we never seemed to be in danger.

Aimée went by bus to Pacific Valley School down south for a while, and made some new friends. John Sabateur was designing a whole new line of clothing for the Phoenix Boutique. My social life was being filled out with new friends who introduced me to making astrology charts, giving tarot card readings, and studying Eastern mysticism. A new spiritual identity was emerging. I was put in contact with someone from Florida who could "read" my past lives. There were frequent buying trips to the Pilgrim's Way bookstore in Carmel as I pursued a new spiritual path. Bill Tache, one of many local gurus working as a waiter at Nepenthe, advised me to wear patchouli oil and carry crystals to ward off evil spirits. Of course, there was also moonlight dancing on the terrace to Creedence Clearwater, sipping martinis at the bar, huddling at the huge outdoor fireplace, and drinking wine while sitting on pillows that lined the stone bleachers.

I was enjoying my new life at Nepenthe, and forgetting the pain of my Big Sur beginnings. One night in particular stands out. A beautiful silver cross—encrusted with pearls, red coral, and green turquoise—had caught my eye at the shop. I saved up my paychecks until I could buy it. When I wore it, adorning the long red velour dress made by John, I decided to celebrate my elegant purchase with a steak dinner, and drank too much wine. Lolly told me later that I had solemnly sworn to them that I didn't belong to a witches' coven. They were simply amused at my confession, and gently put me to bed somewhere. And of course, Aimée was somewhere I was not. Someone, much more responsible than I, was caring for her, along with some other parent-less children. And that was probably either Lolly or Mary Belle. That didn't seem to be much of a problem in those days. Single parents were set free to pursue their fancies.

For example, my destiny was strangely altered one evening when a young man introduced himself to me as Krishna. He said Ellen, my Berkeley folk-singing buddy, now living in Los Angeles, had sent him to me as a gift. I was both flattered and intrigued. Meeting Krishna, whose real name was Fyador, proved to be an unexpected turnaround in my life. He looked more like a Russian prince than a Hindu god, with a round smiling face, swimmer's shoulders, and long dark hair. Ellen had regaled him with fantastic stories about our Berkeley folk singing days, and he seemed so excited to meet me. Though surprised and delighted by his attentions, I never bothered to learn his last name. After one wine-soaked moonlit tryst, I let him know I wasn't interested in a long-term relationship. Deeply wounded by betrayal, any real intimacy terrified me, so I avoided him. He stayed around Nepenthe for a while, but since I didn't want him making any demands on me, he left as quietly as he had come. It was easier that way. He could remain a phantom memory, and I, a free spirit.

Some weeks later, while taking a bath, I sensed in my body that I was pregnant. The realization was both warm and chilling all at once. I hid my secret for a week or so, until I had to share the news with someone at the shop. One woman was sure I needed to get an abortion, since I hardly knew the father, and no attachment had been formed. Then, my career at the Phoenix gift shop was just beginning to blossom, and she offered to do it for me privately, using knitting needles. Her suggestion that I unknit this little being from my womb seemed so cruel that I hid my heart's recoil from her.

Meanwhile I reveled in my burgeoning breasts and body. Modeling clothes on the terrace was becoming so much fun. I wore makeup for the first time in many moons and my hang-loose hair was curled into some glamorous hairdo. Wearing lovely dresses and jewelry I could never afford to buy masked the pain of disillusionment with life. I basked in the adulation of tourists and staff after working hours, and felt safe in the company of charming homosexual men who wanted only dance partners. The child growing inside me gently nudged me to embrace another chance at motherhood. Slowly a desire to simplify my life, and start all over again, welled up in my soul. It seemed that my redemption was at hand.

Chapter Three

Winds of Spiritual Change

Spirits *are like winds that can lift us heavenward, or shake us to earth like leaves falling from a tree. Some winds are dark and chaotic; others swirl around us peacefully, and gently wake us from our dreams.*

In the late 60s a whirlwind called Arica Institute was blowing through Big Sur. I remember talking with a lovely English girl, one of Jeff's dancers, about the latest spiritual buzz. Marianne was convinced that Arica's teaching was what Big Sur really needed. Knowing I was a seeker, she asked me a penetrating question, "Mary, what is it you are searching for?" The answer came much too swiftly, "peace of mind." And there it was, naked and newborn from my mouth. I knew it was the truth. My soul, the deepest part of me, was at war with the universe, locked in the torment of being cast out as a wanderer like Cain, and marked by God for all but me to see.

Oscar Ichazo, a Bolivian-born mystic, had gone into the desert of Arica, Chile, searching for answers to the basic questions of life. He emerged with a strategic vision for humanity's enlightenment. In Argentina, he had met with various shamans and spiritual guides to form a group that was later named the Arica Institute. Now a revered master himself, he continued to spread his esoteric gospel until it reached the shores of Big Sur. Many of the South Coasters, especially Jeff's group, had bought into his mixed bag of disciplines, based on Sufi mysticism, Gurdjieff, and a smattering of Tantric yoga. They had left Point 16 and relocated at the DeAngulo Ranch on top of Partington Ridge, funded by the rich son of a toymaker. Roland Hall had gone to Chile to be initiated into the group. He started an Arica-style Retreat at the ranch with his new soul mate, Melanie. (*Later on I learned that these two had died within hours of each other, attended by some of Irene and Bill Wiesjahn's children who had been caring for them.*)

Wherever Arica's system of "Psychocalisthenics" was taught, relationships usually changed partners, and minds went careening over cliffs. Jeff soon found a new amour, a sweet young girl named Peaches. Carol had given him another child, who sadly had been brain-damaged by the lack of oxygen at birth, while Storm attended as midwife. Jeff wasn't able to be a father though, especially to a needy child. Carol eventually had to leave Big Sur seeking help for her baby. Jeff's mother, Kitty, who was an expert in educating children with special needs, may have been able to offer advice and resources. Once more, Raymond would have to play the surrogate father to another one of Jeff's children.

Ichazo, a compelling charismatic figure, had stated that he wanted to train young Americans how to gain an advanced spiritual state, without the use of drugs. Soon he had successfully planted his Institute in the heart of New York City. A group from Big Sur's Esalen Institute and Berkeley, including Jeff and company, followed him there. In reality, Arica had become a playground for wealthy seekers who wanted to unplug from the Western mindset and explore Eastern horizons, in a safe, sexually charged and supposedly drug-free, haven. However, the hippie culture eventually succeeded in exporting their wares into this group and they, led by Ichazo, experimented with a variety of psychedelics.

At first, Ichazo denied that he was a guru, but then later he reportedly proclaimed himself to be an avatar, in touch with the "Ascended Masters" who had given him instructions on how to save humanity from self-destruction. Smaller groups still practice his disciplines in America and England. Aricans usually have a yearly reunion on Maui to hear from the "Lord Ichazo." Oscar and his wife Sarah have retired there, and live in a golden monastery where he still continues to write books.

Soon, the Nepenthe grapevine was shaken by another spiritual wind. Baba Ram Das was coming to Big Sur. It thrilled me to learn he would be conducting a spiritual retreat at the home of Jan and Joan Brewer. Several years earlier, I had seen him speak alongside Timothy Leary in Berkeley. His name then was Richard Alpert, a Jewish lawyer who had been turned on by Leary, and had become his more straight-laced partner. They rode the circuit of student-packed meeting halls together, urging our generation to join their revolution for higher-consciousness, which we did with wholehearted abandon.

Now he sat there, bronzed, head shaven, and cross-legged on the floor, dressed in the saffron robes of a Buddhist monk, gathering disciples around him. I could scarcely believe my eyes at his transformation. He had gone to India, and found a guru who could guide him in his search for enlightenment. After he had achieved a certain spiritual state, he returned home to Boston where his parents met him at the airport. With a typical Yiddish inflection, he described their reaction to his new identity with typical Jewish comic relief. "Is this our son the lawyer that we sent to Harvard?" We laughed along with him at their dismay and confusion. We had all experienced this to some degree within our own families. Before we joined this sacred circle, we were advised to drink some tea laced with acid in order to communicate with him on the same plane. Each of us carried a question that burned deep in the soul, and now had a place to be voiced. He answered each one without hesitation, looking quietly at the person as he spoke. He seemed the epitome of a holy man, one I could learn from, and even follow.

Soon it was my turn. "Can you tell me where I can find the Christ?" I didn't realize this would be my question until I actually voiced it. Then he asked me, "What path are you following?" I whispered, head lowered, "I am worshiping the sun." "Good!" he said. "You're on the right path. Keep going until you find a golden door. He is waiting just behind it." I murmured a polite thank you, and lowered my head to the floor. I can't describe the joy I felt then, knowing I was on the right path and that I would at last find Him who was searching for me. That intensely mystical moment was forever marred when I saw Ram Das sometime later, still in saffron robes, leaning against the bar at Esalen, having a beer. After he had fallen off my personal pedestal, and joined the human bog, I could never pursue spiritual kinship with him. At that time, I remember carrying a copy of *The Prophet* by Khalil Gibran, the Lebanese poet, and resonating with his message. The image on the book cover had stirred my soul, though I didn't realize then it reminded me of Jesus. I was strangely filled with peace, and ready to take the next step into motherhood.

One evening at Esalen, I met a pregnant, golden-haired young girl named Kelly who told me that Bill Wiesjahn had recently died from a drug overdose, and she was carrying his child. She introduced me to a woman there who wanted to rent us her cabin at Mill Creek, some twenty miles south of Esalen. Kelly and I agreed that we could easily share the living expenses, so we both applied for food stamps and welfare assistance. The social worker that interviewed me looked sadly mystified when I told my tale of an absent father whose only name was Krishna and who had vanished into the great unknown. I knew that this was a cheap shot, but was grateful for the temporary help.

And soon Aimée and I were on the road, hitchhiking again, with our bundle of belongings. We said goodbye to Nepenthe for a season. Kelly and I joyfully set up housekeeping in an authentic 19th century cabin, furnished with a couch, table and chairs, an imposing wood-burning cook stove, a loft where Aimée and I slept . . . and no running water. It was still spring, and we put in a small garden, carried water from a nearby stream for our needs, foraged for deadwood, and even sawed off branches to maintain the fire. Luckily someone heard of our plight and brought us firewood.

Across the highway from us was a small beach we visited, where Aimée could play and collect shells. Rising up behind the cabin, like sheltering arms, were the Santa Lucia Mountains, green and thick with trees. I showed Kelly, who was only nineteen, how to crochet hats and make flannel blankets. We often hitchhiked to town for groceries, and an occasional doctor's visit. Our biggest adventure was walking a few miles down the highway to a place called Lucia Lodge, chatting with the locals, being ogled by the tourists, and buying hot chocolate or a piece of homemade pie.

One evening as we walked past the glowing sea at sunset, a long-forgotten Italian song, "Santa Lucia," suddenly came to mind.

At first I sang it softly to myself, and then out loud with delight, because I knew at last who was growing inside of me. Her name would be Lucia Claire, which meant "clear light." Of course! The name Lucia was echoing all around us! In the following months, life would be reduced to a sweet simplicity, and a quiet waiting for little Lucy to come.

Chapter Four

※

Becoming a Big Sur Mama

Kelly was such a strong, independent person for someone so young. Though only about 19 years old, she took sharing her life with ours in her stride. I enjoyed her laughter so much. It became a warm welcome music in our home. Her narrow blue eyes almost disappeared when her strong white teeth curved into a broad smile. Watching her as we planted our garden together was like seeing a vision. She wore long white pants, and brushed off any dirt that clung to her hands. The delicate movements of her long golden hair while seeding the earth enchanted me. When I knelt down next to her, my own approach seemed so primitive. I loved getting close to the earth on hands and knees, as if I were bowing down to elemental deities, blissfully unaware of spoiling my appearance. This earth-born passion for watching how plants grow and produce food has never subsided. It would overtake me as I dug out furrows for planting, frantically burying the seeds and patting the earth down. I could hardly wait for the first green shoots to appear.

Kelly was a different kind of South Coaster, who had recently come from a newly formed Point 16 set. Her "old man," Bill Wiesjahn, had survived as its caretaker until he carelessly mixed heroin, speed and booze into a fatal cocktail, and was found dead in his car near town. She always spoke kindly of him, and it was comforting to know that he had ended his days in her lovely company. We had both been surprised by our pregnancies, but were eager to begin a new chapter in our lives.

Our days were spent shamelessly hitchhiking to Esalen for the baths, to Lucia for Mrs. Harland's pie, and to Nepenthe for Lolly's wonderful Ambrosia burgers and french fries. Once, while visiting there, someone told me about a woman named Lois about to give birth alone without any midwife available. I felt immediately that I should help her, and got a ride to her home where I found her well into labor. Because I was a stranger to them, she and her husband Bob asked me to leave. I started to walk away perplexed because I felt I had been *sent*. Then Lois called me back, and I did my best to comfort her as she gave birth to their first son Joshua. I was frightened to see how blue and limp he was at birth, but Bob calmly massaged him, breathed into his mouth until he cried and turned pink. This amazing shared experience of God's tender mercy began a sweet enduring friendship.

Monterey was the closest city, but sixty miles from our cabin. We had to do laundry there and shop for basics like rice, beans, lentils, flour, oil, and an occasional portion of meat. Lacking refrigeration, we were usually limited to choosing tuna fish, canned ham, or frozen beef. Kelly found a spot in the ice-cold stream just outside the cabin, and rock-lined it to hide our milk cartons. As the weather grew colder, someone brought us coal to use for heating and cooking. That meant the daily search and cutting of wood could cease for a season. I also visited a doctor there who monitored my pregnancy and was horrified to learn that I was planning on a home birth, instead of enjoying the amenities of the fabulous hotel-like hospital in Carmel. My last visit was auspicious. He said the baby had not yet turned, meaning the head was not engaged in the birth canal, and pleaded with me to stay in town. His concern was that I might have a breech birth, which would be dangerous for both the baby and me. Poor Doctor Rydell! He was one of the best doctors in town, but part of "the establishment," so I chose to ignore his counsel. This made him very angry, and we parted in the throes of his frustration over having to deal with a stubborn hippie mother. But I was determined to have as natural a birth as possible, because I had been denied that with Aimée.

A poet friend named Andy had offered to drive Aimée and me

to town, on this particular visit, and we welcomed his kindness. We had met at Esalen, and he was very drawn by the mystique of our Big Sur lifestyle. Andy had a cabin up the canyon on the old Coast Highway Road, which he offered to share with us, if the need ever arose. The fullness of my pregnancy should have weakened me enough to allow someone to care for us. But I was fixated on this home birth becoming my baptism into the circle of Big Sur women. He graciously settled into the role of protector and companion.

As we drove home that afternoon, we decided to take a rest stop at Esalen, and have some dinner. I felt very tired, and was having some light contractions. A doctor who was attending a seminar there seemed very concerned to learn of my circumstances. He had never been at a home birth, and asked me endless questions. My answers were vague and nonchalant because I didn't really know what to expect myself. After dinner, he invited Andy, Aimée, and me to rest in his room. When it was time to go, he wanted to talk with us about a dream he had while we were all sleeping. He said I was going to need help when I went into labor, and to please contact him when it was time. Andy promised him that he would. I felt strangely comforted by his concern. The dream's message lay heavily on my heart.

A rainstorm was brewing as we arrived home with all our goods. We put things away, and made a fire in the stove against the chill. Kelly came home soon after, and we talked about what to do when the baby came. I had prepared a clean sheet to put on the couch, and told her to be ready with blankets, towels, and hot water. She too had never been at a home birth and was understandably a little nervous, and I forgot to tell her about the doctor's dream. Andy settled down on the floor in his sleeping bag. Aimée and I climbed up to the loft went to sleep.

A few hours later a small rush of warm water awakened me. My labor had begun, and I quietly lit the kerosene lamp. The cabin was dark as everyone slept. I reached for *The Prophet* and began reading and silently praying for the child about to be born. The pains became more intense. I called down softly to Andy, and told him it was time to get the doctor. He left swiftly, and drove like a madman fifteen miles in a heavy rainstorm, past mudslides to reach Esalen. It was a little after three a.m., and still dark. I climbed down from the loft and carefully carried the lamp over to the table. Kelly awoke and helped me stoke the fire. I wanted to eat a healthy breakfast, so I prepared liver and onions. She laughed at my choice but knew I needed strength. So we ate together, and Aimée came down to join us, and was excited to hear the news. Soon, I couldn't stand up any longer, and my breathing became more intense. I motioned to Kelly to get the couch ready for me, and I lay down. I could hardly speak at that point. She frantically asked me what she could do to ease the pain. I placed her hand on the small of my back, and asked her to massage it.

The earth moved away from me, and I labored in an oceanic kind of consciousness, where waves began to overwhelm me. I didn't see the door of the cabin fly open or the doctor rush in. He called out to me, dropped his bag on the floor and put on his gloves. The baby was presenting breech, and he saw her little legs dangle from me. He rushed over and felt for the cord around her neck. He gently pushed it away, and helped ease the baby out. I saw a little round face with bright blue eyes shining up at me, and I called out her name, Lucy! Aimée held the lantern as her sister was being born. It was January 14, 1970, and dawn was just about to break open the sky. I watched the pale blue light turn into a golden shade through the window, shimmering on rocks and trees around us. I wept with joy and gratitude for the amazing mercy of her birth. Andy watched reverently from the shadows. Surely, Lucia's arrival had been noted in heaven, and protected here on earth.

Aimée thought another child was coming when she saw the placenta leaving my body and happily announced, "Mommy, here's another one!" We were glad it wasn't true. Kelly asked me what to do with it, and we decided to bury it in the garden. The doctor cut the cord, and Lucy was ready to be diapered and wrapped up tightly for me to finally hold. Kelly helped me to clean myself as the doctor watched in fascination. He was thrilled to have been a part of this miracle, but was concerned that I might need stitches. I remember trying to stand up, even though I felt faint after the blood loss. Still I insisted on trying, after putting some heavy pads into clean panties Kelly had given me. The act of giving birth supersedes every other reality and removes all the normal barriers of modesty. In a daze of wonder and joy, I picked up a five-pound jar of honey I had bought for us to share as gifts. I wasn't able to hold it, and it dropped, spilling the mass of honey all over the floor. Andy valiantly salvaged as much as he could, carefully separating the pieces of broken glass from the ooze, put it into a smaller jar, and offered it as a thank you to the doctor. He silently accepted it.

Soon Aimée, little Lucy and I were bundled into Andy's car and headed for town. We dropped the doctor and Kelly off at Esalen with the latest headline story to tell. It rapidly rolled down the Big Sur pipeline, punctuated with many exclamation points. The miraculous tale of Lucia's birth soon found a home in many a wondering heart.

Our reception in town was one of mixed reactions. Dr. Rydell was so angry with me at first for ignoring his counsel that he wouldn't see me. A young British doctor named Whitworth took pity on us and examined Lucy for me, pronouncing her normal and healthy. He then spoke to Dr. Rydell and convinced him that I needed medical attention. Soon I was in his office, receiving the stitches I needed. He even asked me how the birth went. His demeanor was politely aloof, but was still obviously uncomfortable having to treat a hippie mother who had been a very noncompliant patient. He probably disliked everything I represented: an independent spirit, a complete disregard for normal conventions, and a naive trust in Mother Nature. But he was not alone. At that time home births were not welcome in the medical community. And certainly, the social mores of Monterey and Carmel were perched far above the fray of countercultural ideas.

As fate would have it, Dr. Rydell became my gynecologist and surgeon many years later. He removed an ovarian cyst he'd found, and didn't remember the drama of Lucy's birth when I recounted it to him.

Somehow in this mix I met a nurse who was entranced by our home birth experience, and talked Aimée and me into staying with her for a week. She wanted to use me as a shining example of a successful natural childbirth and for the joys of breastfeeding among the several pregnant women she was instructing. Andy was amazed again at this turn of events, and dropped us off at her home. For one whole week our little fledgling family had a blast. We were fed well, cared for, pampered, and trumpeted like native royalty among this eager group of ladies. I was delighted to be on display as a model for a successful homebirth. It fully rounded out my first experience of having been denied that joy with Aimée.

When it was time to head back to the cabin, I called Andy, who had hovered over us for a few months. He drove us back to Mill Creek, and then we gradually drifted down different streams. Many people came to visit us there, just to hear the story from my own lips, and to coo over Lucy who looked like a little brown berry. We would often sit naked outside the cabin, soaking in the spring sunshine. Many times when Kelly and I took Aimée and Lucy to the baths, people would comment on the beauty of my two golden children. Kelly loved to display her rounded belly and seemed to have gained a new confidence about her approaching home birth experience. Our lives had turned a corner into a peaceful valley of contentment. It was good to be counted now among the Big Sur mamas.

Chapter Five

Life Dances in Circles

A nearly idyllic time at Mill Creek came to an abrupt end after one of our frequent visits to Esalen. As South Coasters, we felt privileged to have the nearby luxury of dipping into the hot baths, and enjoying a wonderful organic meal. Kelly came running up to us with startling news, "Ginny wants to move back into the cabin!" Our absentee landlord had been offered a job, maybe even at Esalen, so she and her two daughters had returned and decided to make Big Sur their home. We had only a week to gather our things and find our own place. You can be sure this news rattled the Big Sur Grapevine big time. Poor Ginny! She was cast as the clueless outsider who heartlessly evicted some of Big Sur's own: a pregnant widow and me, a mother of two with a newborn.

A handsome young man named Joel wasted no time coming to call on Kelly. They talked for hours outside on the porch, and she seemed equally enamored. Before we parted ways, Kelly used her clout with the new caretakers at Point 16, and they offered us a place to stay. So we were back again full circle, this time under a new regime. The commune was no longer a nudist camp, a party pad, or a musician's drug scene. The new caretaker cut wood for a living, and raised goats to sell their milk and cheese. He came over to our place one day to introduce us to his prize goat, spotted like an Appaloosa and appropriately named Apple Lucy. He offered us fresh goat's milk for little Lucy, and his gesture seemed a portent of a better destiny there.

We lived in a plastic greenhouse structure, the same one that Jeff had used to make a home with Carol after their first child was born. It was definitely a roof over our heads, but not much more. Our doorway was the ubiquitous Indian bedspread. Our furniture consisted of two platforms: one had foam for a bed; the other held our few belongings. I made our meals in the cabin we called the "big house" where Bill Wiesjahn, the father of Kelly's unborn child, had lived not too long ago. Another season had rolled in on Point 16, which was destined in later years to become a legitimate artist's colony. The huge iron gate made an impressive entrance to some gardens and a few simple structures for living quarters that overlooked the vast shimmering ocean far below. Huge bundles of pampas grass grew abundantly in these parts and gave the place a laid-back, island atmosphere.

Dr. Whitworth, the English doctor who had checked Lucy at birth, came to visit us there. He was the favorite doctor of the counterculture because he supported our natural ways. After examining her he seemed concerned that Lucia had "fallen off the growth chart." He asked me extensively about our eating habits, and couldn't find fault there. I was still breastfeeding, and had supplemented that with some simple foods and goat's milk. He suggested I go to Esalen and seek help. I remembered that Dr. Ida Rolf was living there, instructing students in her deep muscle massage therapy called Structural Integration, or more popularly, Rolfing. Somehow I knew she had the answer to Lucy's growth problem. When I saw this tall, elegant, white-haired lady in a lab coat teaching a class, I sensed that she would understand a mother's desperation. And so, I walked right up to her, holding out Lucy in my arms. She asked, "Mother, what is the matter here?" My eyes began overflowing with tears as I told her that Lucy had stopped growing. She took Lucy from me and promptly pressed hard on her pituitary gland. Of course, Lucy screamed with pain and fright. Dr. Rolf gently gave her back to me and told me, "There now, Mother, she's going to be all right." As I comforted Lucy, I knew her words were true, and thanked her. She then went on to explain to her inquiring students what she had just done. From that day onward Lucy's growth was normal.

During another Esalen visit, a very pregnant Kelly had some startling news to report. "Mary, you won't believe what happened to our old cabin! It burned down to the ground!" I was astounded and asked if anyone had been hurt. "No," she explained that one of Ginny's daughters had left a kerosene lamp lit in the loft, and it fell over during the night. "There's nothing left except the stone chimney and a part of the old cook stove." I was speechless, unable to comprehend that Mill Creek's ancient cabin, once our home, was gone forever, reduced to smoldering ashes. Here was another juicy tale for the grapevine to chew over, and judgment was unanimously pronounced upon the event. This was a textbook case of karma, pure and simple. It was indeed extraordinary, and we seemed to be vindicated in a sense. Ginny and her girls had to make a quick exit from Big Sur, fortunate to be alive, but having lost everything they had in the fire.

Life in our humble domain continued without mishap, except for the discovery of dead rats at the bottom of the well. Luckily I usually boiled our water because we were always drinking tea, or juice and goat's milk. I have a vague memory of becoming a Shaklee Vitamin saleswoman in that era. How I ever got into the business is too deeply buried now, but I do remember a company representative coming all the way from Los Angeles to meet their newest top-selling agent. I had used our plastic tent-house as a warehouse, and was making good money selling the supplements, especially to the Esalen crowd. He was very surprised to find a hippie doing so well, especially one whose living arrangement was so unconventional. Of course he wanted to help out a single mother raising two children, so he gave me a bonus or two. His sales report and his gracious gesture must have raised some corporate eyebrows.

I don't remember much more from that time period except the pleasant feelings I had of acceptance from the Big Sur community. Apparently my expertise in making astrology charts had caught the attention of Patrick Cassidy, a South Coast legend, famed for his moonlight dancing orgies. His piercing blue eyes looked out from under a handcrafted leather cowboy hat, his face shaded with stubble, and he usually wore a leather vest to complete a Wild West look. He loved to greet visitors with a small tin of Royal Jelly, that substance fed by the bees only to their queen urging them to try it because it gave incredible energy. I received a surprise invitation to attend the birth of his latest child, and record the exact time for a chart I would make. Storm was chosen to be the midwife, the role she had secured in South Coast society. Patrick was also an artistic welder, and I noticed an oxygen tank outside of the bedroom window. The child was born limp and blue, and Storm had trouble getting the baby to breathe. As the appointed timekeeper, I knew several minutes had passed, and yelled to Patrick to get the oxygen tank. I told him to blow it just outside the baby's lips, and his little son pinked up immediately. Another miracle of grace had lifted us all from the jaws of death.

I was surviving the rigors of Big Sur, but more importantly, I was actually thriving. Whenever I saw Jeff, in chance encounters at Esalen or on the road while hitchhiking, I felt a new inner strength and a strange detachment from him. I was living life on my own terms now. The terrible bondage of his soul power over me had been broken. The pain of rejection toward his child and me had subsided. From that point on he became a passing shadow on my horizon. Our marriage had been a terrible lapse of judgment on my part, and I was living out the consequences.

There was yet another life circle about to be completed. Don McQueen's wife Barbara had come all the way to visit us just after Lucy's birth at Mill Creek, and I could tell she was concerned for us. One day Don met me at Nepenthe, obviously relieved that we were able to handle the new living situation and the Point 16 crowd. He told me of an opportunity on top of Pfeiffer Ridge to live rent-free in the role of a caretaker. This was the dream job for any hippie, and I was thrilled that he thought I was ready. It meant we would have a place of our own, and become firmly rooted in the community. He drove us three miles up a dusty dirt road and showed us the place with great flourish. It sat high on a promontory, overlooking the ocean in the distance, veiled at times by drifting clouds that hid the immense valley to the west and the little houses tucked carefully among the oak trees and manzanita bushes up and down the ridge. I could hardly believe my good fortune.

His company had landed a plum contract to build a giant aluminum and steel building for very wealthy clients, where money was never a topic of discussion. He talked freely about this very profitable project, spicing his success story with humorous, repeated conversations between him, his boss, and the couple's architect. She was from a prominent Carmel family, and he was a dark and handsome ne'er-do-well with a strange Basque name. They had asked Don to find them someone who could stay on the property until they could move in. This planned building, considered a fiasco in the making, had become the hot topic around Big Sur kitchen tables because the monstrosity had violated the beauty of these surroundings. It looked more like a Bank of America than a home, and was nicknamed the "blimp hangar." An enterprising architect, who had adopted a Salvador Dali persona, had been able to convince this couple not to use wood in order to save trees from destruction. Instead of blending into the landscape, it reared its ugly head like an alien spacecraft that had blasted a huge crater on top of the hill. Its many steel girders seemed to groan in misery, and were already beginning to rust. The couple had indeed purchased a breathtaking view, but only so long as you looked toward the ocean, and avoided focusing on the place where this strange monolith grew out of the earth.

In sharp contrast, our new home was a little construction shack nestled in a grove of live oaks a little further up the embankment. There was a refrigerator and outdoor sink attached to a narrow tool shed a few steps further. Behind the shack there was an unprotected outdoor shower and an outhouse. Electricity ran the amenities on the outside, but only a classic Franklin two-burner wood stove graced the inside. There was a fenced area just waiting to become a garden, and a water spigot nearby with a hose waiting to be attached. Everything we needed seemed to be there. It was definitely a step up for us, and I was ready to move on. Don warned us that winter storm winds could be pretty fierce, and that the rain would sound like thunder bolts on the aluminum roof. I would have to wash dishes outside in all kinds of weather. The shack had no insulation, and the wind was free to come inside and rattle our bones. But it just looked like a little cabin to me, enough for the three of us, and so much more than the see-through shelter we had. Nothing he said could deter me from claiming my little portion of paradise.

Someone drove us down south to gather our things, and Don brought us up the ridge to begin our new life. His company had completed their part of the job by then, so his crew was no longer working at the site. Once again, the McQueens had performed a rescue operation for our little family, and helped us go on. Lucia was almost a year old, and Aimée was nearing age six. Don was one of those gentle giants in the land, and a very successful businessman. He told us about some of our good neighbors who lived below this property: the Morgenrath clan—and numberless people who lived with and around them—Sylvia Rudolph, and her son Byron. Then, to the left of us were a young couple named Gopher and Linda and her daughter Raffi, and just down the slope from us, Ruth and her daughter Jennifer, who was Aimée's age. They all may have wondered about Don's judgment in assigning us this job since I couldn't drive, and would have to depend on help to get the basics for creating a life here. But destiny had propelled us here, and I was energized to make it all work.

Little Lucy, a year-old toddler, sat contentedly on a blanket under a curve of oak trees, playing with rocks and plants. I had to continually chase away the yellow jackets that buzzed around her head, making her cry from fright. Then the biting deer flies constantly assailed us. But Aimée and I went about cleaning up the homestead of nails and forgotten tools, gathering leftover wood for our stove, and pieces of manzanita root dense enough to burn like coal. We had no furniture except a large wooden platform laden with foam in the back corner for our bed. I soon had it covered with Indian bedspread material, and a few odd pillows. Some baskets I had saved were hung from the ceiling to hold fruit, dried branches of rosemary, and leaves of the native mint tea called yerba buena. I scavenged the place and found some gnarled pieces of wood that had been discarded, plopped them in a creaking wheelbarrow along with a handsaw, hammer, and nails. In a few days, I was able to make a table and a stool. This was my first and only venture into woodworking. *I still have the stool, now used for a plant stand, and sold the table at a garage sale.* These two simple pieces came together so well that even my new neighbors were impressed. The cabin had one narrow corner window at the front that became our dining area, and the long wooden box we carried everywhere became our bench. When I lit our two kerosene lamps, coaxed the fire in the stove that was adorned with a big brass gurgling teakettle, and the popcorn was ready to burst in the Dutch oven . . . we were home.

Chapter Six

Haven on a Hill

Aimée quickly made friends with Jennifer, Ruth's daughter, and their little green trailer became her second home. She loved staying there for many reasons: having a playmate her own age, Ruth's gentle spirit, and the trailer, which seemed more like a normal household space. Everything was contained inside, and not scattered in three places. Our cabin was more like a pioneer homestead, so primitive and plain. I had a variety of emotions: a little jealousy at Aimée's preference, yet thankfulness that she had a real friend, and that she was enjoying our new place in the sun.

Aimée and Jennifer became schoolmates as well, and went to Captain Cooper School, a wonderful place for her to begin a real academic life. The teachers were avant-garde in their thinking, and devoted to the arts. The educational system used was primarily self-tutorial, and having early learned to be independent, Aimée soon adapted. She flowered intellectually in this new creative environment. The students made for an interesting cultural mix and clash: some from Nepenthe and others from the Naval Facility at Point Sur. Our kids brought rather healthy lunches that they often traded for the sweet treats their friends brought from the base. Our girls dressed in a simple, country manner, yet often envied the town girls who sported the latest clothes and shoes. Ruth would faithfully take the girls down the hill in her little black truck to the bus stop, and in good weather they would walk back up the steep three-mile ridge, by their own secret trail, making it an adventure for themselves and some hardy friends from Nepenthe, Holly's daughter Erin, and Kim's daughter Nani. I often rewarded their blistering trek with some cookies and cold lemonade.

Ruth became a very important friend in my life in Big Sur, and a further bridge for me into the community. She was a beautiful lady with flowing long black hair, and a disarmingly gentle sense of humor. Ruth had been working at Nepenthe as a chef for a while, and was well-known and well respected. Her connections varied widely: from Carmel, where her mother lived, to the folk-singing circles of Monterey and Palo Alto, and now to Big Sur. She confided that Judy Collins owned the property where her trailer was parked. To my disjointed psyche this put her in a different league, a celebrity crowd of real "somebodies," while I was still a "nobody," struggling to overcome past mistakes. One day, after looking at some family photos, she smilingly told me that a life-sized nude photograph of her had been hung in a museum. That caused me to wonder if I ever could have had the courage to do that, or if I would have been worthy of such a portrait. I had stopped looking at myself since my Nepenthe modeling days. A mirror just wasn't a part of our belongings or even part of my thinking. Perhaps I couldn't really face myself, because my very identity was in question.

Another dimension of her life was revealed when she introduced me to her lover, a young, vivacious woman who was a talented photographer. She had an acerbic Jewish wit, proved to be delightful company, and loved to fuss over my two girls, snapping pictures of them on the ridge and at Nepenthe. I am forever grateful to her for taking the only photos I have of Lucia's childhood, since Aimée had been much photographed in our earlier Berkeley days.

This was Big Sur, a place where everybody went, and anything goes. *Why was this so difficult for me to assimilate?* Ruth had seemed so normal, I thought, and I immediately labeled myself as someone who had sexual hang-ups and quaint ideas. Because I was so disconnected from the real world, having a camera seemed so materialistic. Living literally in the Buddhist "Present Moment," I had not really valued the idea of preserving memories of Aimée and Lucy's childhood. The girls had no toys to speak of, and our clothes were hand-me-downs from the overflowing freebie box at Nepenthe, or an occasional visit to a local Goodwill in town. Even so, a barely discernible distance developed between Ruth's household and me. Whenever I stopped by to visit, my awkwardness prevented me from really enjoying their company.

Helen Morgenrath, who lived further down the ridge, soon took on our need to shop for groceries. She was a sun-kissed mature woman, still beautiful, strong, and vibrant in her looks. Her blond hair was beginning to show signs of graying, her bright blue eyes danced and twinkled with such a merry light, and her smile spread over her whole face, full and sweet. Helen always managed to effortlessly pack both my groceries and me into her small, trusty, ever-dusty car. We constantly chatted about the latest items on the vine as we drove together. She must have helped me with my laundry as well. Most of the natives went to town once a week or so for a big laundry day. Helen also taught me much about Big Sur folklore, naming plants, and pointing out herbs and their uses, while sharing the history of the earliest settlers. Once she showed me a bush outside our cabin that she called soap lilac. Indians had used the blooms she said, and showed me how they created a sweet-smelling lather when rubbed between the palms. You can be sure I used them when I took my shower the next evening. She had taught me how find yerba buena tea in the woods, and where an abundance of huckleberries grew hidden under the manzanita bushes along the ridge. I eagerly absorbed these nature lessons.

Helen possessed the kind of strength I could admire, someone who had survived a divorce, and was raising her family on this ridge with class and gusto. She was transforming her dustbowl of a homestead by planting grass, flowers, and luscious vegetables. I was also delighted to learn that she taught modern dance at the Big Sur Grange Hall, the community-meeting place. As she taught us dance movements, and exercises, her body morphed into that of a young girl's, and she was definitely suppler than I was. It was a soul-refreshing experience for me and the other ladies who came. Ballet was like poetry in motion, and I felt cheated at not having an opportunity to learn this art as I grew up.

Usually the only male present at these classes was a tall, gaunt, curly-haired man named Pasha. He looked as if he belonged to an

Indian sect, and squeezed himself into a corner, sitting in lotus position, out of sight, and only spoke in monosyllables. Helen was not embarrassed by their live-in arrangement, but he seemed to be a little uncomfortable. She introduced him to us by his name, and added no other tag or title to their relationship.

Helen had a strapping young son named Helmuth who was somewhere in his early twenties, and who volunteered to help me put in a garden. He brought up a load of mushroom compost, mixed with Big Sur's rich black shell mound, a gift deposited by the ancient Esalen Indians who had once hunted abalone along the rocky shores and left their shells to decompose, enriching the earth. I set to work planting everything Helen recommended: Swiss chard, tomatoes, zucchini, onions, green beans, eggplant, and melons. Outside the rusty link fence, I created a curtain of mammoth Russian sunflowers to beautify it. I was ecstatic when everything was finished. This added so much life to our homestead, and I devoted hours to nurturing my vegetable babies. In the small curve of oak trees outside the cabin I planted an herb garden of comfrey, oregano, and basil. It was edged with rocks I had gathered from around the ridge and loaded into my trusty wheelbarrow.

Jali, Helen's youngest son, was an angel-haired boy who looked like a Rafael painting. Her two daughters were Celia, a dark-haired honey of a girl and newly married, and Tara, a lean blond beauty like her mother, who became a friend to Aimée, and initiated her into the hippie culture by piercing her ears in the acceptable homespun manner. First, she numbed her ears with ice, then pierced them with an ice pick while holding a cork behind each lobe. Aimée was thrilled to show me the circles of string she wore, waiting for her ears to heal, and asked if we could pick out some earrings from the Phoenix shop. She was growing taller, stronger, and lovelier each day, and seemed more content with our lifestyle. The one thing children will always be able to do, no matter what their circumstances are, is to play and enjoy life as it comes to them. It was a brief season of contentment for our little family. *Had we finally found our niche in paradise?*

Chapter Seven

A Stone's Throw from Hell

All the love that surrounded us, and all the help we received, did not quell the turmoil raging inside me. Something was terribly wrong with this picture of paradise. There was no one at my side, helping me, no prince with whom to share this tiny kingdom. The romantic part of my life seemed to be over, though I was still in my prime. My thoughts swirled between the beautiful fantasy of living on top of a mountain, and my bitter daily grind as a single mother. How could I possibly take care of these two precious children, alone, without a husband and a father? My emotions were put on hold. My heart's fire was reduced to a few small embers, and I was haunted by a loneliness that draped itself around me like heavy mourning clothes. What had first been a haven for our family was slowly becoming a hell on earth.

Aimée slept peacefully unaware beside me. I was thankful she still enjoyed the innocence of childhood. Lucia slept in a little closet she liked to crawl into, which I curtained with some checkered blue and red material. I would always play a wooden music box for them at night before they went to sleep—trying to create a fairytale atmosphere—and often sang lullabies. They didn't have to know about my inner sorrows. It was so precious to see Lucy wake up in the morning with her feathery hair standing straight up, looking like a fairy creature, and asking me to go potty. Instead of going to the outhouse at night we used a round blue bowl as a chamber pot that I hid under the bed. Of course I was the chambermaid, and emptied it discreetly every morning. Ruth and Jennifer got a kick out of our little Victorian tradition.

That was also the time I decided to buy Aimée a horse. She had been born with an insatiable desire to live on a ranch and ride horses. It seemed so strange that horses had never been a part of my upbringing. Mother had said someone in her family had once raised Irish race horses. Maybe that was the connection. Anyway, I met a woman who was selling a Shetland pony named Jingles, complete with saddle, for a very reasonable price, so I bought him. Of course Aimée was thrilled and she and Jennifer preferred to ride bareback between our houses. It also meant I had to buy hay, have it delivered into a small corral that didn't yet exist, all of which I knew next to nothing about, and needed help even to accomplish. But my heart's desire has always trumped my ignorance. It may have seemed only a foolish gesture to many, adding yet another burden to our lives, but I was thrilled to be able to give such a valuable gift to Aimée. She had been deprived of so much at my hands, I felt. I hadn't anticipated Jingles becoming the neighborhood nuisance, wandering up and down the ridge, and eating from their gardens. He would also play an important spiritual role later on in my history. I tried to keep him tethered and corralled, but often forgot to do so. Life was becoming a maelstrom of wants and needs, of impossible dreams and unwelcome nightmares.

My spiritual state was much darker than my emotional one. The following truth is still difficult for me to face, let alone confess: I seriously wondered if I had been sent there for the purpose of being a contact for spirit beings or even aliens. Every evening I put out some food in a wooden bowl in front of the cabin window, as an offering. I spoke aloud to those beings I imagined wandered among the trees, telling them I was friendly, and would not hurt them. It was all done without fear, except that of being discovered doing this before I had made contact. Of course the food was gone in the morning, thanks to the raccoons and squirrels. That fact had never occurred to me, and I never told anyone about these evening activities until many years later. Eventually I gave up because I received no answer, and the darkness became more threatening by its very emptiness.

In the early mornings I would find an isolated spot, sit in lotus position, and gaze at the rising sun. This was supposed to create a body of light within me, and help me gain access to the astral plane that existed somewhere between heaven and earth. It was a peaceful exercise though, and again, I did it secretly. I didn't know then that a sect in India meditated on the sun continually, and its adherents eventually went blind. I hungered for the supernatural realm, and out-of-body experiences, as an escape from normal drudgery.

Through the years I had accumulated books on the teachings of Gurdjieff, the Sufi Mystics, the Ascended Masters, and other occult studies. Bill Tache who worked at Nepenthe had put me in touch with a medium in Florida who did a series of life readings for me. We corresponded often, and her letters sketched a curious mixture of the past person that had formed me into who I now was. She said that I had been part of the Berber people living in North Africa, and a keeper of books in the Library at Alexandria before the great fire. These fragments hinted at some familiar threads of meaning, but still left me without purpose or a coherent vision for my present life. Often while washing dishes outside, my mind would be fixed on a series of labyrinthine exercises for controlling my thoughts, designed to awaken in me a greater depth of consciousness. I was *working on myself,* a technique taught by Gurdjieff. It was supposed to bring me peace and tranquility, but instead it had hardened me into adopting a stoic attitude toward life. My usual *joie de vivre* had evaporated into a deep melancholy. My primitive lifestyle had forced me into daily battle against the elements and elemental spirits. A residue of bitter waters was at the bottom of every dream, every well of repose.

I was losing control in another realm, one that happened during a dream state commonly known as "astral travel." These journeys began to increase in number, and unnerved me; so much so, that I had to drink wine before I dared go to bed. I longed for the oblivion of unconsciousness, a self-induced stupor. During the rare times when I smoked pot, it re-created the devastating effects of LSD's dreaded leap beyond the portals of sanity. I would be caught in a mental vise, for fear of losing my mind completely. During astral travel I seemed to be serenely floating above my body, and at other times something seemed to be chasing me into a dark corner, and I would feel suffocated. My soul had been loosed from its moorings, and the silver cord that held it, broken. I would wake up in a panic, and calm myself with another glass of wine. My nights were far from being restful.

One night in particular exploded into a real confrontation with the dark side. The veil to the supernatural realm was parted for a split second, like the blink of an eye. What I saw turned my life inside out. A huge monstrous spirit, laughing insidiously, was throwing my soul around like a rag doll, against the walls and the ceiling. The terror of this reality caused my soul to quickly reenter my body. I lay on the bed, awake, but barely breathing. And my response to this horror came inexplicably from a deeply buried place. I lit a candle near me and began to whisper the name of Jesus, over and over, like the desperate prayer of a child seeking comfort in the dark. I hadn't spoken that name for many years, except in angry curses. I looked at the flame for a long time until I felt peace fill the room, and soon fell asleep.

The next day, and many days after, I would carry this moment with me, not daring to share with anyone. Who would believe what had happened anyway? It only underscored the fact that I was a crazy woman, and caused me to retreat further into isolation. I even entertained thoughts of suicide, a desire to leave what was becoming a place of torment. I was trapped again. My ignorance was the cause of my undoing. I had thought that the levels of white witchcraft I was practicing dealt with good spirits. After all, I was participating only in the fun stuff, like giving tarot readings, wearing patchouli oil and energy-catching crystals, consulting mediums, and drawing astrology charts along with their interpretations, which was my forte. These methods of divination had given me a modicum of power, and actually bewitched me into thinking I had gained enough knowledge to control the present and to see into the future. I wasn't interested in learning spells, or belonging to covens, the heavy black arts; that kind of power scared me. But now there was no escape, no exit from the hellish room I had furnished with a dangerous delusion of goodness and light. Confronting the true face of evil had broken the spell, but I had no remedy, no potion to regain power over my will, over my soul. My outward life continued as before, but inwardly my mind had been unhinged.

Then I bumped into something even more mysterious that really troubled me. One morning I had gone to Ruth's trailer to borrow coffee for my morning ritual, and noticed she was surrounded by a strange-looking group of visitors. They had driven up to her place in a wildly painted school bus, and seemed intent on staying. (*I later found out that they were labeled "Jesus Freaks."*) Ruth seemed unusually anxious as she introduced me to her niece Kathy, who was traveling with them. As I took the coffee from her hand I quickly turned and ran back up the little trail to the cabin. Everything in me wanted to escape their eyes, and the way they looked into mine. There was another kind of light in theirs, and other fire that threatened to consume what was left of me. It was much later I came to understand that what was happening to Ruth that day was to change our lives forever.

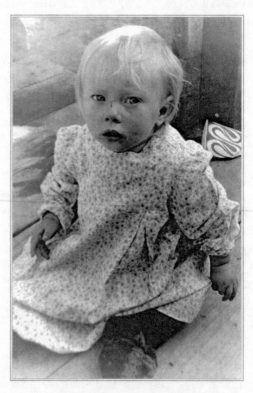

Baby Lucy playing on Ruth's porch

Chapter Eight

Knocking on Heaven's Door

The first thing I noticed after the "Jesus Freaks" had left Ruth was that Jennifer came up to our place to play more often. She and Aimée had made a seesaw out of a rough plank and a rusty oil barrel. What a picture they made of childhood innocence and beauty, bouncing up and down, their blond hair flowing like wings around their shoulders. They were laughing and singing songs. I heard strange new words: "Mt. Zion, beautiful for situation, joy of the whole earth, City of the Great King." I started wondering about God again. Who was He and where did He live? And of course, Aimée wanted to stay at their house even more. Then came a blow I'll never forget. One morning Aimée looked at me pleadingly and said, "Mom, this is crazy. Why are we living this way?" She was only seven years old, and saw something I couldn't yet see. I was shamed into silence, because I had no answer for the question that kept ringing in my ears.

Ruth began to visit me more frequently, too. I was delighted at this new interest in our lives. She seemed so much more peaceful, someone to whom I could confide my spiritual troubles. I wanted to understand why a spirit had come in such an unloving, aggressive way. One day as she and I were sharing a cup of tea, I told her about the visitation. I felt I needed to explain to her first how spirits from the dead often wandered among us, needing to extract the essence of a living person in order to remain on earth longer. Ruth listened very quietly, looked at me, and lowered her eyes. She said, "No Mary," shaking her head firmly. "Dead people's spirits don't wander around looking for our essence. They don't come back that way, if at all." I was hardly breathing when I said, "Well then, what was it?" What she said next, leaning closer to me, almost in a whisper, came crashing down on my heart "That was an evil spirit trying to harm you, Mary." My inner world was instantly shaken apart by fresh waves of terror. Our conversation may have continued but I don't remember any other words. But before we parted she said something to me for the first time, "I'll be praying for you."

Her final words made me glad because I was in trouble and needed help. Ruth seemed to know so much more about spiritual things than I did, and I began to trust her wisdom more. Once when we were visiting with Helen, she walked by me and said offhandedly, "Did you know that God loves you so much that He has numbered the very hairs of your head"? These were no ordinary words, because they melted into the core of my being, and hung as a presence in the air around me. It was like an unexpected embrace from an invisible person, someone I hadn't met. At the same time, the power behind them unnerved me, and I began to wonder more about this loving God who still seemed so distant from me.

One Sunday afternoon in February 1972, I was listening to a radio program from Berkeley, my old stomping grounds. We had a portable radio and tape recorder from the Goodwill that had a microphone attachment and a mini sound system. The girls used it to make recordings of their songs and stories, and it proved to be the best toy I could have ever purchased. They spent hours creating dramas, and recording Lucy's sweet babblings. Aimée and Jennifer had gone to Ruth's for a visit, carrying Lucy with them, and I was left alone to take care of our pony. I had tethered him to one of the oak trees outside the cabin, hoping he would be satisfied grazing on the grasses there because I had again run out of hay.

An unknown preacher was telling a story from the Bible about Abraham and his son Isaac. Mysteriously, God had asked him to sacrifice his son on top of a mountain. Even though I was a former Catholic, I knew very little about the Bible. So I was fascinated, and chose to ignore Jingles, who was neighing for my attention. I kept telling him to "wait a minute" until I finally heard the surprise ending that I understood even less than the story. God called out of heaven for Abraham to stop, just before the knife plunged into his son Isaac. He pointed to a ram caught in the bushes as a substitute for Isaac, and Abraham killed it as an offering to God. Why would God have asked him to do such a terrible thing in the first place? It was all so confusing. But I finally yelled to Jingles that I was coming.

When I walked outside, I stepped into a time warp. Everything dissolved into dreamlike slow motion as I stood gazing at the place where I had left him. A beam of sunlight had illuminated the stand of gnarled oaks, revealing a scene of horror. Jingles had wrapped the rope around a tree in frustration, had fallen helplessly against it, and had broken his neck trying to get free. The rope was tight around his tangled mane. The air around him was very still except for some flies buzzing around his head. I fell to my knees in shock, gasping with grief at the sight of this dear animal. It had all been my fault, and I started sobbing. It was then that I heard a voice that was both audible and distant, coming from another world. God, who had spoken to Abraham in that story, now spoke directly to me. "Stop now, or something more terrible will happen!"

The voice hadn't told me to stop weeping, but to stop *everything,* especially the direction in which I was headed; in effect, to stop living what I had known to be life. It was a Divine intervention of such magnitude and a flashpoint of such terrible warning that my time on earth has been forever measured before and after that moment. I saw the lives of my innocent children hanging in the balance. Now I was weeping from the deepest sorrow I had ever felt, and trembling from the deepest awe I had ever known. God Himself had come to stop me in my tracks as surely as I had been born. How long I knelt there or if I ran screaming for help, I don't remember.

Somehow I made my grief known. The girls came running up to see me, and they screamed hysterically when I pointed to where Jingles lay. Their beloved pony, strangled to death! Only hours before he had been alive and stubborn as ever. They ran to tell Ruth, and stayed in her trailer with Lucy while Ruth went to get Helmuth, Helen's oldest son. He and Jali drove up almost immediately with a backhoe, and buried Jingles near the garden. I couldn't watch.

His death had caused a spiritual tempest to rush upon me in such fury, that I was left desolate, humbled, and clinging only to a voice. Those words still echoed in my spirit, and mattered now more than anything. No one knew what had really happened, and they couldn't understand why I was taking it so hard. They left me alone to grieve, and I walked over to the mound of earth that now covered his body. As I knelt on it, still unable to control my tears, the words of a childhood prayer poured out of my mouth. "Our Father, which art in heaven . . . forgive us our trespasses. . . ." My lips trembled as my heart bowed down in sorrow for my sins. I prayed with an assurance that my words were heard and with a new awareness of their real meaning. Jingles' unmarked grave became the burial site of my old life. A wayward daughter had come home to her Father.

Later that evening Ruth came to bring Aimée and Lucy home. She could sense by my countenance that something supernatural had happened, and asked if I would like to come to a prayer meeting. At first I mumbled a very solemn yes; I thought I was ready to step into the world that she had recently entered. Then, inexplicably, I put my hands on my hips and said defiantly, "Whoever is strongest gets me!" I was a little embarrassed by my response but thanked Ruth for inviting me. *Where did that strange voice come from, I wondered.* It definitely had been beyond my control. Before I put the girls to bed that night, I tried to explain to Aimée how I had been changed by Jingles' death, and accepted full blame for the accident. She seemed to be comforted, and able to muster a smile through her tears. I don't remember if we prayed together, but sleep that night was like a balm poured over my tortured soul.

The next morning Jennifer came to cheer up Aimée, and they sang songs as they rocked back and forth on the seesaw. They would often hoist Lucy up on the board with them, much to her delight. That day I moved slowly around the cabin, drinking deeply of the new mercy I had received but did not yet understand. Life no longer seemed a heavy burden I had to carry, but more like a reprieve from prison. That evening Ruth arranged for the girls to be babysat, probably by Tara, Helen's daughter. She drove up in her little black truck, and off we went to the meeting.

While driving there I remember babbling like an idiot because I was so afraid of what I may or may not have become. I had to make sure Ruth knew I wasn't the Virgin Mary, or Venus, or any such illustrious spiritual entity. She must have bitten her tongue quite often, trying not to frighten me any more than I already was, during our ride up there. I'm sure I was in a confessional mode about my occult experiences. I didn't know who I was yet, except that a huge God-moment had just happened, and life seemed to have drifted into a never-never land, somewhere between heaven and hell.

I followed her into Tom and Sue's cabin, lit only by kerosene lamps, and murmured hello to everyone before I sat on the floor. These were Ruth's closest friends and though I hadn't met them, they knew all about me from the grapevine. I was entering an entirely new circle of life. They were well-known singers and musicians. Tom started a song on his guitar, and Rita joined him, then Ruth. I can't remember which song it was, but I do remember a Presence coming into the room as they sang. It was the same Jesus I had loved as a child, the one I had clung to in Holy Communion. This was not what I was expecting. I watched Him move slowly toward me. "He's here," I said in a whisper, and fell on my face, weeping. The singing stopped and someone asked, "Who's here, Mary?" wondering if I were seeing a demon. "It's Jesus; it's Him! He's really here!" was all I could say. They seemed to understand what was happening to me, and their beautiful voices and soft music melded everything into His Presence. Time was suspended into an eternal embrace as I bowed at His feet, washing them with my tears.

This was a homecoming I never imagined could be mine. I was like Mary Magdalene worshiping at the feet of my deliverer and Savior. In a brief moment, the beauty of Heaven transformed my little space on earth into a peaceable kingdom. This is where I would live from now on. The ten long years of searching for a Master, the Christ, had finally ended. His name was Jesus, and He had rescued me, one of his little lambs, lost, bruised, and bleeding, the constant prey of ravening wolves. I was safe in his arms now, and I would never let Him go.

Chapter Nine

"Like the First Morning"

When Ruth left me at our little cabin later that night, I was still in a state of shock. During that first meeting, despite the calm, gentle folk songs and friendly hugs, I couldn't stop crying. Tears of anguish rolled like years of rivers from my swollen eyes. I was both ashamed and undone. Bumping into Jesus, of all people, had not been on my spiritual radar, or part of my agenda. The dark spiritual world I once wandered in had been violently overthrown by this loving Shepherd. This was a paradigm shift of immense proportions. Jesus? Just Jesus? Could it really be that simple? What about all the disciplines I had practiced? All the knowledge and all the books I had acquired? How could I explain this to my oh-so-very savvy friends? Nothing I had done or had thought of doing could have prepared me for this radical departure from Big Sur's cultural norm of an all-inclusive spiritual equation. My inner world had been rocked beyond recognition.

Ruth did not leave me empty-handed. She gave me a Bible before she said goodnight, and helped me gather the girls into their beds. Soon I was by myself again, nurturing the kerosene lantern, and reviving the fire in the stove. But this solitude wasn't an aloneness anymore; it was filled with the presence of another, closer to me than breath, and yet distinct from me. Before me was a book I had never even considered reading and certainly not ever purchasing. I dusted off some branches of yerba buena that hung from the rafters in baskets, made a pot of tea, sat down at my crude homemade table, opening it to the book of Genesis, the book of beginnings.

It was like dipping into a warm, salty ocean, immense and inviting all at once. Since then, reading Genesis has always washed my mind from the crusty barnacles of spiritual indifference and renewed a sensitivity to the mystery of our origins, and the intentions of a loving God. After all, it was God who searched for Adam hiding in the garden in the shadows of his sin. It was God who hovered over chaos and turned it into the cosmos, an orderly world of stunning beauty, like a necklace of jewels.

And surely I had been found hiding out in my own earthly paradise. But now I had been washed from sin, head to toe, and all of nature with me. The morning of a new world had broken in upon us. We were perched on top of this dry thorny ridge, where clouds surrounded us like warm wings. Spring had infused the atmosphere with the beautiful oleander fragrance of Big Sur. I walked to the spot where I had once worshiped the sun. This time I bowed my face to the ground, and wept at my former ignorance of the One who had made the sun, moon and stars. These were now my fellows in creation, and no longer deities I had to appease. I greeted the Lord of creation and asked forgiveness. Everything around me whispered His Name, and I joined the birds in their chorus of praise. Jesus had come to live in our little shack on the mountain, and had made it a holy place. My little ones were safely enclosed in a new household of faith. We, who had been orphaned and cast aside, now belonged to the family of God that extended over the whole world.

That afternoon, I shared my adventures in Genesis with Ruth. There was that gentle, knowing smile, and a shaking of the head. "Better not start there," she said. "Too complicated. Better to start at the Gospel of John, and learn all about Jesus!" Her words pierced me again. She was right. I knew so little about this Jesus who had rescued me. For so long He had been a mysterious being imprisoned behind the golden tabernacle doors in a church. Childhood images vanished as I learned about a Jesus who existed before time, the eternal Word spoken by the Father in creation, and who became our flesh and blood brother, living among us as God incarnate. John's Gospel began in a similar Genesis style that revealed His true identity. Waves of healing light flowed over my once tortured mind.

A whirling vortex of new thoughts began to emerge. Suddenly the radiant personage of Jesus overwhelmed me and filled the universe! I saw Him as the axis of this earth, and the living substance of all creation. He was the Eternal Logos, the Word still speaking everything into existence. He was the true light guiding me on my way, His way. Every other path I'd followed led nowhere; every other light I'd known paled in comparison. This was so exciting! All I could do was bow my heart in wonder. He was so much greater than I could ever have imagined! I also felt a little cheated and upset with the Catholic church. Why hadn't they taught us who Jesus really was? Why did they hide Him from us all those years behind a tabernacle door? I still had to learn that the Holy Spirit is the One who guides us into all Truth, and that any earthly institution, whether religious or scientific, can only know in part something of this immense reality, the foundation and ground of our being that we call Truth.

I walked around the ridge, both awestruck and love struck. The daily grind of chores: gathering twigs and roots, fussing in my garden, washing dishes outside, or making soup on my little Franklin stove, was transformed by new meaning and purpose. This invisible lover of my soul whispered endearments to my love-starved heart. He had lifted up my head, once bowed down with shame and guilt, and turned my bitter springs into a fountain of joy. I had been translated from a dreary scrub-oak life into a realm of heavenly beauty, and it seemed that I had regained the true Paradise of God, that which Adam had lost. Now perfection was in reach, maybe just around the corner. It was a delight to visit Ruth and her daughter now. Instead of confusion, there was a spiritual fusion built on the shared experience of a loving God who had visited us both, and turned our lives upside down.

But I hadn't been sprinkled with angel dust or become an ethereal being by any means. True, smoking pot and the desire for drugs had just vanished. I merely chuckled when my vain attempts at cultivating a small marijuana plantation failed after I promptly forgot to water. Still, the desire for cigarettes held me in a vise. It was a crawling-in-the-mud kind of slavery, bringing me to my knees to pick up butts from anywhere so they could be re-rolled when I wasn't able to buy any. And then there was the evening glass or two of Spanish sherry that dulled dark memories, and helped to quiet the storms of sexual fantasy that would assail me at times before I could sleep.

When Ruth prayed for me in a strangely beautiful language, I felt new courage. I asked her what had made her pray that way, and she said it was a gift God had given her and I could have it too. She excitedly explained that if I wanted it, I was invited to come as we all went to a special meeting in Carmel.

Chapter Ten

"They Sang a New Song"

Going to these prayer meetings in town may be the first time, that I can remember, that all of us, Tom and Sue, Ruth, Rita, and all six of our children: Sue's two boys, Chad and Gabriel Sunrise, Ruth's Jennifer, Rita's Ben, and my Aimée and Lucy piled into their VW bus. Those were the days of no seat belts, and we all squeezed in together just fine, bouncing around like happy pilgrims on an adventure. In fact, in those unfettered days, Big Sur mamas often nursed their little ones while driving! To our twenty-first century eyes and ears, this probably seems foolhardy, but it was truly a feat of engineering and positioning—as was the slippery navigation of steep, dirt roads in winter rains, in a car or truck packed with laundry or wood for the stove, groceries for a month, and children playing tic-tac-toe in the back seat! All this was accomplished with ease and daring-do, in the pioneering spirit of Big Sur families.

The first evening we walked into Fred and Beverly Upham's lovely home in Carmel in the spring of 1972 was such a treat for us. We were enveloped in the warm golden light of electric lamps, clean upholstered furniture, colorful rugs, and welcoming smiles. This fellowship of Charismatic Catholics met to pray and study the Bible together and allow the Holy Spirit to move freely in their midst. They were thrilled to meet our little group of hippies from Big Sur, and they wanted to know how God was moving among us. But we were there to receive from them, and learn what God was doing in the larger Christian world.

First of all, God was saving Catholics and filling them with the Holy Spirit, an outrageous affront to the Protestant world, many of whom were convinced this was a doctrinal impossibility. God was moving through mainline denominations, upsetting current theological apple carts, and He was especially delighted in the 70s to remind us that He is no respecter of persons or denominations. And here we were, a marginal group of people labeled the "unchurched," that God had chosen to be witnesses within a very closed artistic community. That evening proved to be a fruitful cultural and spiritual exchange. We had all come with hungry, expectant hearts, eager to join with this loving circle of Christians as they prayed. I was happily swept along by a gentle river of the Spirit, as some prayed, others sang in different prayer languages, and finally, we all joined hands in a new song: "We are one in the Spirit, we are one in the Lord; and we pray that our Unity will one day be restored; and they'll know we are Christians by our love, by our love, they'll know we are Christians by our love." This was how it should be, and what was missing from church life, I thought. I never wanted that song to end.

Someone prayed for me to receive the Baptism of the Spirit, and I felt a warm stirring in my spirit, and heard new sounds come out of my mouth. We were all drinking from such a deep well of joy there. Many people spoke words I had never heard before, all from the Bible, as if God were speaking directly to them, and then to us. They were shared like treasures suddenly discovered and we received them as if they were personally chosen gifts for us. It was as though a faucet had been turned on that became a torrent of life-giving water.

We were all encouraged to share our hearts, our needs, our revelations, and most of all: how we met Jesus. It was hard to leave such a vital spiritual atmosphere that first night. It seemed I had been transported to an advanced state of sanctity, but then one of the first things I asked was if anyone had a cigarette on them. I was so ashamed of the chain that still attached me to nicotine. It would take another year before I was free from that addiction. How I longed to be strong spiritually, and really free in every possible sense of the word.

Ruth often visited her mother's home in those early days with us in tow, and Jennifer, Aimée, and Lucy prattled joyfully like chipmunks. We talked about how great it would be if our girls made their first Communion together. So, Ruth arranged for the ceremony to take place in the Carmel Mission. I remember frantically making a flowing white dress for Aimée, and watching with teary-eyed delight as she and Jennifer knelt down at the altar. Still, I never thought about rejoining the Catholic church. There were too many doctrinal muddles I couldn't resolve. And yet these familiar rituals had power to enthrall me with their mysterious beauty.

Living on Pfeiffer Ridge had taken a whole new turn when I started singing and playing the guitar again, after so many dreary years of silence. Music began to choke out all bitter roots of sorrow, and a new joy filled all the empty places in my heart. One evening, after burning the little blue notebook of poetry I had kept from the Berkeley days, I asked the Lord to give me His songs instead, written in this new language of truth and hope. And as I prayed and sang to the Lord in the nights that followed, a musical miracle actually began to happen.

"Reveal me, Jesus, to my soul. Oh, heal me, Jesus, make me whole," were the first words to pour out of the new me. Of course it was awkward to share my song with such a fine group of musicians, but they graciously received my beginning efforts. I could hardly play the guitar without trembling, or sing without weeping. Ruth, Tom, and Rita had inspired me whenever they shared their new songs. Thus began the continuous outpouring of music and song that became a hallmark of our little group. Though my hands and voice still trembled, and tears of joy flowed freely, I stepped happily into this musical circle of life glowing with golden sounds.

Chapter Eleven

The Jesus Revolution

Tom and Sue had graciously opened their home to our little meetings on Partington Ridge. They were an extraordinarily beautiful couple that could easily have been movie stars. Tom was a talented guitarist and songwriter, and Sue a gifted craftswoman. They lived in an iconic Big Sur cabin on property that may have belonged to Tom's family. He was also an outstanding carpenter, and built a beautifully crafted house for goats that we all wished we could live in! They and Ruth and Rita had first heard the Gospel from a visiting friend and fellow musician named Paul. They all sang gospel songs together, and he witnessed to them how Jesus had transformed his life. His testimony caused them to investigate a Christian commune called The Lighthouse in northern California.

These first seeds of faith sown into their hearts helped prepare them to embrace Ruth's extraordinary experience. Tom and Sue's simple lifestyle and loving family seemed an ideal to which we all aspired. Sue's son Chad went to Captain Cooper School along with Jennifer and Aimée, Holly Fassett's children, Erin and Kirky, and Kim Rowe's children, Cappy and Nani. They were an inseparable band of ragamuffin bohemians in those carefree days, and often took the long dusty walk up the hill to visit Ruth and me. It made me so happy to see Aimée really enjoying school and fitting in so well with her new friends.

Our group was growing in number as more people heard about what had happened to Ruth, and the "Jesus Freaks" who had visited her that fateful day. She was still working at Nepenthe as a chef, and was respected as a well-loved daughter of the land. But her testimony had definitely rattled the Big Sur grapevine, causing not a few tongues to wag and heads to shake in disbelief. They heard that she had ended her love relationship, was seen reading her Bible constantly, and was now sharing her experience openly. There were some who listened, amazed, and wanted to know more about this Jesus, but others didn't want to be associated with those Jesus Freaks whom they considered to be wild and wooly radicals.

Another group, called the Children of God, had wandered into Big Sur around the same time. They were known by the impressive amount of scripture they had memorized, would quote long passages to anyone who would listen, and seemed harmless enough. However, their leader, David Berg, gradually led these lambs to the slaughter, and formed them into a notorious cult. He was renamed Moses David by a group of devotees he called the Family. It was later reported that he seduced many virgins, molested many children, including his own, while still proclaiming he was a Christian. Berg had indeed been raised in a devout family, but had been twisted by the power he wielded over so many sincere seekers of Jesus. He was one of many self-appointed prophets who grossly perverted the Christian message in those early days of the Jesus Revolution.

The Jesus Movement was, in effect, a radical return to the basics of Christianity, and had succeeded in overturning the culture of "Churchianity," or the status quo of church life in America. Young people left the dead churches of their parents in droves, in search of deeper spiritual reality. Ruth herself had once been drawn to the Bahá'í group, which believed Jesus was only one of many Divine Messengers sent by God to bring mankind into unity and maturity.

Others in Big Sur were disturbed and even angry with the new Ruth for breaking rank with the traditional neo-Buddhist philosophy, in which sin was not considered the fatal flaw of human nature. Searching for truth had simply been a personal matter, and certainly not an issue of life and death. But Ruth's life-changing experience, much like Saul of Tarsus meeting Jesus on the road to Damascus, had transformed her so completely that it became the catalyst for birthing a spiritual movement that would slowly overturn the tables of our laissez-faire lifestyle. This new society became known as The Big Sur Fellowship, an authentic first-century style Christian community, springing up like wildflowers among the majestic redwoods of the Ventana wilderness.

I remember sharing my own experience with Helen, and was so excited to tell her that I had reached the state of enlightenment or Buddha's Nirvana. Her face changed from delight to confusion to dismay as I explained that Jesus, the Light of the World, was now my Master. Her reaction made me sad, because our friendship became strained after that. My zeal to impart this joyous encounter with God and my newfound relationship with Jesus had overtaken any bounds of reason and especially wisdom. I continued to meet with skepticism from some friends, and it became clear that I had crossed a spiritual and cultural dividing line and didn't know how to handle it. As a newborn Christian, I had no idea what it meant to be a follower of Jesus, or how I should behave among those who had long harbored animosity toward Christianity, had thought it suspect, or those who had strange misconceptions about Christians.

While at Nepenthe one day I told someone how Jesus had changed my life while holding a martini in one hand and a cigarette in the other. He listened politely but concluded that I might be one of the "chosen ones" but that he wasn't. I tried to explain that Jesus came for everyone, not just for a special group of people. The truth is that our hearts have to be prepared like garden soil for the rain of God's Spirit, so that the seed of eternal life, His word, might take root and grow. *How many times had I heard the Gospel, and hadn't responded?* Of course, our ways, our conversations, and our lifestyle were all slowly changing, and further differentiating us from the culture of Big Sur. We desired more and more to be with each other, to talk about the Bible, to understand the person of Jesus, and to be pleasing to God.

That summer Helen had worked hard, along with her sons,

to finish her beautiful swimming pool, surrounded by grass and flowers. It was a magnificent addition to the ridge, and we were all invited to come and enjoy it, and we often went swimming nude. Later on, it was awkward to explain why we came wearing a bathing suit of sorts. How could we explain that it was nothing anyone had told us to do? That it was the Holy Spirit living within us who was constraining us? The veil of an illusory innocence had been removed, so we could see that we were sinners, along with everyone else we knew.

I had been born again by the Holy Spirit when I asked Jesus to come into my heart. Contrary to all that I had previously been taught, I learned that God doesn't automatically live within you; you must invite Him to come. Jesus Himself made it very clear when He said, "No one can come to me, except the Father draws him." Since God respects the sovereignty of our will, we are free to respond or reject His wooing. I certainly had turned my back on Him, yet He never stopped pursuing me, even as I ran headlong into the mouth of Hell. Whenever I thought about His humility and long-suffering throughout my years, how He looked beyond my stubborn pride, my cold-hearted rejection of His Love, how He longed to heal the deepest wounds of my heart, I would weep inconsolably.

But now I was so happy Jesus had saved me that I wanted to tell everyone in my family, especially my mother, the good news. The former construction workers had installed a telephone in the tool shed; one that I scarcely remembered was there. So I called home, trembling with excitement. "Mom, your prayers have been answered!" I yelled into the receiver. "What do you mean, Mary?" she said quietly. "I've been saved and filled with the Holy Spirit! She moaned and asked, "Oh no! You're not one of those holy rollers are you?" I had forgotten that she equated Pentecostals with the kind of people she had seen writhing on the sidewalks of New York City. Nothing I said after that could convince her that this wasn't the case with me, even though I described how much my life had changed. Though I had hidden from her much of what I had been through after meeting Jeff and his family, she felt sure I had crossed over into enemy territory. She knew nothing of the drugs I had taken, or the occult teachings I had embraced. It would take twenty years before she would be somewhat reconciled to the fact that her daughter had become a Protestant. She saw me as a traitor to the true faith, even though she herself had married a Lutheran. Of course my phone call was unwise in its timing and wording, but even so, I cried like a baby over her rejection.

Having lived for so many years in fantasy and deception, I was still oblivious of how to behave normally in the real world, the natural world of flesh and blood people. I couldn't understand why others close to me hadn't reacted with joy to such good news! Like so many of us in the early days of our fellowship, I was a woman deeply in love with Jesus, my heart and mind captivated by the lover of my soul. Much later, when I read the C. S. Lewis novel *Till We Have Faces*, I understood more fully what had happened to me. Lewis used the myth of Cupid and Psyche to describe how the interior world I was experiencing was really invisible to others. As long as Istra lived with the god of Love to whom she had been given as a sacrifice, she was forbidden to look upon his face. Their humble dwelling was nothing more than a shack to others, but to her it looked like a magnificent palace, glorified by the god's nightly presence. It seemed that she could never be lured back to the world of royal intrigues and meaningless ritual. Unfortunately, she was tricked into doubting the reality of Cupid's love by the jealousy of her older sister, and the desire to see her lover's face eventually brought about her death.

Much later in my walk with Jesus, I felt moved by the Holy Spirit to burn all my books on occult teachings, not knowing there had been a similar incident described in the New Testament. This was an expensive collection I had purchased mainly from a bookstore in Carmel called Pilgrim's Way, and had gathered through many years of searching for the truth. These books now seemed worthless to me next to the Bible. I also had been made acutely aware of the dark side while gaining this kind of spiritual knowledge. Practicing some forms of white witchcraft had actually opened up a Pandora's box of information about covens, witches, and warlocks. I knew that a human sacrifice was required for their meetings every Halloween evening. The members were also intent on calling up evil spirits, and even Satan himself. Everything in me then shrank from any form of witchcraft, and I wanted nothing more to do with such practices, or such beliefs. I knew firsthand that evil spirits could deceive us into thinking that there was really no harm in experiencing the chills and thrills of exploring the supernatural realm.

When my book burning became known, it caused a strong negative reaction among many Big Sur people, and remarks were made about the book burning done by Nazis. Then I learned that another sister, named Eileen White, did the same thing to her vast collection, so it must have seemed like a strange group activity, even though I had never heard of anyone else doing this. The main criticism we heard was that these books could have been given to others, and not destroyed. To our way of looking at it, preserving them would have been like spreading a disease, and we couldn't in good conscience do that. There were no more trips to the Pilgrim's Way. Since we needed to understand more about this newfound faith, we all bought our books, music and teaching tapes, and tracts from a small Christian bookstore in Monterey.

Another innocent impulse caused further misunderstandings and even some indignation on our ridge. I had the idea of putting up Christmas tree lights in the form of a cross on the huge glass wall of the "blimp hangar." Some brave brothers climbed onto the roof, and lowered the lights onto the surface. And there it was, a huge shining Cross of light that could be seen for miles. We were thrilled, but some of our neighbors were outraged! Perhaps they thought we were establishing a church on top of their mountain. The building was enough of a monstrosity, without having the Jesus Freaks claim it as a place of worship. All we wanted to do was proclaim Christmas as Jesus' birthday, and that He had come to live among us in Big Sur. The lesson we learned is that the Cross is always an offense to those who don't accept who Jesus is. As I recall, it was promptly taken down the following evening, but Pfeiffer Ridge had earned a new nickname: Jesus Hill.

People began showing up at my door, as the news spread about this growing group of Christians. Barbara Woyt, new to the land, and ready for adventure, came asking for a place to stay. She was related to Nate Saint, one of the five missionaries who had been speared to death by a headhunting tribe in South America. An aunt, one of her relatives came to visit, making sure Barbara was in good

Christian hands, not knowing then that her niece was struggling with her faith. Both Barbara and I were relieved that she left us, sufficiently satisfied.

Barbara was an amazingly energetic young woman who taught me how to make "Ezekiel bread," by grinding sprouted wheat berries into dough. She later became famous for her skill in baking all kinds of bread and cakes. One day when the old barn at Ventana, with a newly established restaurant nearby, was being torn down, she went there immediately to salvage the redwood shakes. It appalled her to hear they were being thrown into a woodpile to be burned, and she got help salvaging them, and brought them to our little homestead. We began nailing them on like shingles, acting as a layer of insulation over the thin redwood boards. The construction shack was transformed into a fairy-tale house with a charming rustic character. We were delighted that it looked as if it had been on the ridge for centuries. But Barbara soon left us to find her own place in paradise.

Wes, a new brother in the fellowship, had offered to build us a loft, as an addition to our place, and it slowly began to look like a real cabin. He also saw other needs, like enclosing the outside shower with plastic walls, so we had some privacy, and putting a door on the outhouse. Aimée was thrilled with all these refined changes, and rejoiced in being more civilized, like her best friend and neighbor Jennifer. It also meant that she and Lucy had a real bed downstairs, and their mother had a private space in the loft to sing and worship God.

Then a delightful young girl named Annie came to live with us for a season, staying in her van. Her quick sense of humor and warm embrace of our family endeared her to us all very quickly. She was Bill Fassett's niece, and the cousin of his children, Griffis, Dorcas (who was living in Pacific Grove and later became a Christian), Kaffe, Holly and Kim (who was part of our fellowship along with her husband John). Her conversion caused quite a stir within the Nepenthe family. God was indeed directing his attention to that iconic place where many others would come to accept Jesus. *But I'm getting ahead of myself.*

Carol, a lovely young single mother searching for God, came

to Big Sur because she had heard about a band of Christians who knew and served the Lord. Like so many of us, she was raised as a Roman Catholic, an experience that had left her dissatisfied. She had a shy little girl named Stephanie—we all learned to call her "Stevie Ann"—who was about the same age as Aimée and Jennifer. Carol immediately found a job at Nepenthe and was introduced to some of the new Christians working there. Within six weeks she had given her heart to Jesus and joined our growing fellowship.

Soon Carol wanted to live and be with fellow Christians. She made a little home in the tool shed that sat on the other side of our outdoor kitchen sink and refrigerator. A small happy family was sprouting up all around us. Carol worked part-time cleaning houses, and worked with Tom's brother Crile at the Ventana deli. She later moved down to a trailer, sparing her from the perilous drive up and down Pfeiffer Ridge. There she became good friends with Eileen White, a brand new Christian sister who worked in the health food store. Eileen was the niece of Emil White, a renowned Big Sur artist. She and I had been astrology buddies in the past, but now walked together in the Kingdom of Light. Thanks to Carol's diligence and her amazing energy, she was able to find work for many young ladies in our Fellowship, and we gradually earned a good reputation in housecleaning among the locals. It became a signature form of employment for me and many other women in the years to come.

Lucy and Stevie Ann at meeting on Partington Ridge

Chapter Twelve

"When the Veil Is Taken Away"

Our Fellowship meetings were about to change drastically through a young woman named Rachel. She had broken her leg when riding a bike down a steep hill and needed a stay in the hospital. Though Rachel had not yet given her heart to the Lord, she knew about our group in Big Sur, and talked excitedly to her visitors about a group of hippies getting saved. An English lady and two young Christians from a Salinas fellowship were visiting the hospital and met her. They wanted to hear more of what Rachel had to say. The woman said her husband had been praying fervently for such a miracle to happen. And he had been taking some young men backpacking into the hills for months, hoping to meet some of these strange creatures and tell them about Jesus.

Rachel described how a fellowship of Christians met regularly in a cabin on Partington Ridge. She was tremendously talented in singing, and when Rachel eventually gave her heart to the Lord, she added wonderfully to the group's worship music. Because she had been in a love affair with a well-known sculptor who had no intention of letting her go, Rachel became emotionally devastated by the struggle to leave him. Our family of believers rallied around her until her heart was healed.

Meanwhile Tom, Sue, Rita, and Ruth had been praying for God to send us a Bible teacher. Our meetings were growing in number, and there were so many new questions we couldn't answer. But one thing was sure. We may not have known much about the Bible, but we sure loved each other and welcomed everyone who came. It didn't matter whether they were merely curious, or just wanted a meal. We were caught up in something so mysterious and beautiful. Jesus was living among us, and we wanted everyone to know the truth about Him, and why He had come to us in Big Sur. Tom's brother Crile, his sweetheart of a wife Arlene, and their four children had come to live with Tom and Sue at the homestead. They had been saved in a revival in Southern California and were delighted to join the family of believers. Up until then, they had been following a strict regimen from Ohsawa's Macrobiotic philosophy, but Tom and Sue gradually helped them to accept a more balanced way of eating. We saw amazing changes in them and their children, both physically and spiritually.

I have such wonderful memories of us sitting on Tom and Sue's hillside lawn of thick kikuyu grass and listening to "Oh Happy Day" sung by a black gospel group called the Edwin Hawkins Singers, sharing community potlucks, and celebrating Easter Sunday with an egg hunt for the kids. It seemed that we had found a true paradise, and our feet hardly touched the earth. A loving circle of friends surrounded us now, and my children finally had a safety net, especially from me.

Once, when going to pick up Aimée and Lucy at the cabin, Chad came running to tell me that Aimée had fallen from a swing and broken her arm. What I said next was a perfect example of how our iniquities, our inherited tendencies to sin, can overcome us. The first words out of my mouth were, "How the hell did you do that?" These cold-blooded words were exactly what my mother had yelled at me when I had broken my arm. I was so ashamed and horrified that I knelt down right there and sobbed. Poor Aimée was in pain, but my first response had been to think about myself, and the inconvenience of having to go into town. One of the brethren helped me get her to the hospital, and prayed for me to conquer yet another iniquity that had surfaced. Thankfully, the break wasn't too serious, and it healed quickly, though Aimée suffered an emotional hurt that took much longer to heal.

When Donald and Florence Abbott first showed up at our quiet folksy meeting, we didn't realize they would slowly upset the spiritual apple cart. Don entered the cabin quietly, and sat down on the floor. He wore a red wool sweater that Florence had knitted for him. His hair was thinning, but still had a blond patina, and his face sported a ruddy English complexion, crowned by a prominent nose. She was a petite, neatly groomed English lady who seemed so out of place. He made no comment after our meeting ended when he introduced himself and Florence. We were very unsure of them at this point. After attending several of our meetings, he offered to bring a Bible study if we wanted. Since we had been praying for a Bible teacher, we agreed for them to come the next Thursday evening. We knew we needed guidance and had so many questions from our personal times of exploring the Bible. Here was a mature Christian minister willing to instruct us in the ways of God. It seemed that God had answered our prayers.

Our meetings had always been quiet and reverent, much like the ones we attended with the Uphams in Carmel. We spoke in tongues, prayed, and sang the worship songs the Lord had given us, allowing God to direct us by His Spirit. Very often, I would feel something like fire over my head, and God's Spirit would bring words from scripture to my mind, or else give me a direct message. It would take me awhile to obey His prompting, because I was still wounded inside, and lacked confidence.

There were never any programs we followed. Our door was open to everyone: the spiritually hungry, the seekers, the doubters, the curious, and the cautious. People were free to come and go as they pleased. Of course we were always eager and excited to share our personal experiences with anyone who would listen. We definitely had a very informal and quiet style of worship that seemed to fit our surroundings and our lifestyle. It came as such a shock when I overheard Donald Abbott say once after a meeting, "I haven't come to worship the spirit of Mary!" Of course we weren't actually worshiping Mary. We truly worshiped Jesus as the very center of all our lives. And His presence in our meetings was so precious. I had forgotten all about the Mary thing, and there it was again. Looking at English history, from the days of the first Queen Elizabeth, the illegitimate daughter of Henry the Eighth—who had watched her father split the nation into two opposing camps when he appointed himself head of the Church of England—there has been suspicion and animosity toward Catholicism in general, and Mary in particular.

But we never had any qualms about going to those Charismatic Catholic prayer meetings with Ruth. They had been our first family of believers. However, the quiet reverence we displayed in our meetings made him wonder about our roots. Our meetings were definitely not his style, and didn't fit with his theology. But his visits were usually cordial, and we could ask him about scriptures we needed to understand. He also spoke with such authority and conviction, and answered so many questions we had about what it meant to be a follower of Jesus. He never laid laws upon us, but always seemed very respectful of what God was doing among us, and he trusted the sovereign work of the Holy Spirit. That trust impressed me more than anything he could say or do. He often said that what God was doing in Big Sur was unique to our culture there, and we could tell he genuinely enjoyed hanging out with us natives.

However, Big Sur seemed to foster a very subtle elitist culture, and our attitude toward outsiders could be just a bit condescending. There was a need to protect our way of life, and the beautiful land we had inherited, from being sabotaged by those less "spiritually aware" than we were. We were used to visitors longing to be a part of our community, and looking upon us as favored individuals. And Donald Abbott seemed to be just such a "square," someone who could never understand our rogue origins and strange philosophies. Some of us may have felt we were doing him a favor by letting him join our circle, and only later realized how much our ways offended him. For example, it never occurred to us to pay for his gas every week. He finally had to mention it to Tom. Only then did we begin to cover his travel expenses.

Don Abbott and his wife Florence had become Christians later in life, while living in Ghana where Don worked as a diesel mechanic, overseeing a shop. They had been mentored by some American missionaries who lived there, and who later sponsored them to come to America and attend an Assemblies of God Bible College in Springfield, Missouri. Before Don graduated, he and Florence had often taken teams of student evangelists to New York City where

David Wilkerson had begun his work among the drug addicts and street gangs. Wilkerson asked Don and Florence to start a Teen Challenge ministry in San Francisco. After a time of working with Dave, they began praying for a new direction, and had left the ministry of Teen Challenge.

Soon they traveled across the United States as evangelists ministering in Pentecostal churches. Don had been dismayed at the Church's response to the growing "hippie problem." He saw that most congregations would not open their doors to these hippies. The churches didn't want these dirty, smelly, strange-looking young people to sit in their pews. A window of opportunity opened for the Abbotts to start a new work in Salinas, California, through an interdenominational coffee house ministry called "Youth for Truth" that reached out to troubled teens. A small group formed around them and they rented a house where some of the young men, just getting off drugs, could receive spiritual guidance by actually moving in and living with them.

Because Don and Florence were still very English in their speech and their ways, they stood out in a crowd. They were very charming and charismatic and seemed to draw the young, the disillusioned, and the disenfranchised around them. They looked past the drugs, sex trips, and prostitution and saw the hunger for truth, so their ministry was aptly named. Later they rented an old Victorian house they called "The Philadelphia House," which became a gathering place for new converts and served as the first "brothers' house" where young men could be discipled in the Christian faith. A few sisters' houses were established even later, but for the same purpose. After Don began taking some young converts on treks into the Big Sur Ventana wilderness, looking for these elusive hippies hiding in the woods, the unexpected contact with our little group seemed a miraculous answer to prayer.

Our first introduction to their Salinas group came one evening when Don and Florence brought some members to our meeting on Partington Ridge. We were learning to call each other "brother" and "sister" by then, the greeting Pentecostals commonly used within their spiritual family. Some members from Big Sur intensely disliked this new custom. They felt that it caused a loss of intimacy between us in Big Sur, and seemed to them too impersonal and generic. However, I enjoyed gaining entrance into this larger family. The quiet atmosphere changed instantly when Sis. Abbott prayed out loudly in tongues, and then gave an interpretation of a message from God. Personally, I was delighted to hear a woman pray with such passionate abandonment, though many of our brethren and new visitors weren't so sure. The room began to explode with the sounds of different people praying loudly, and some calling out to God with deep yearnings and groans. Bro. Abbott and some brothers gathered around me to pray, sensing I needed deliverance from oppression.

They were right. I did need prayer, because there were times I walked under a dark cloud of shame and fear. No one knew about the demonic encounters I still endured because one never walks away from the devil's playground, free and clear. Some of his hooks remained in my soul and only earnest prayer could remove them. At night, just as I was about to fall asleep, a spirit would pounce on me, pressing me into the pillow, trying to smother me, so that I couldn't even call out Jesus' name, except inwardly. Of course the Lord was with me, and I clung to His presence until I actually could speak His name. The spirit would depart, but always left me shaking with fear, a reminder there is a realm of evil. This is a very common form of demonic intimidation, and evil spirits hope their victims won't say anything, or bring the events to light. They feed upon the fear and torment as their bread. I wasn't strong enough yet spiritually to do anything other than hope they would go away.

It isn't possible to explain what happened when they prayed for me. Suddenly I was no longer conscious of their words, the room, or the people around me. God's Spirit had swept me away into an ecstatic union with Himself. In such an intimate moment, I didn't want others to be gawking at me because I felt so naked before everyone. Bro. Abbott explained that I had experienced a mighty meeting place with God, and there was no need to feel embarrassed.

Later that evening Sis. Abbott looked into my eyes and said, "My dear, you have no character." Her bluntness both hurt and stunned me. It was probably God's antidote for any pride or importance I might have been feeling. She simply looked into my soul and spoke the truth. Because I had been reduced to such a vegetative state through psychedelics, my true identity had been damaged beyond recognition.

The reader must understand that my mind had almost been destroyed by the drugs I had taken and by the spiritual paths I had pursued. I was being lifted out of such deep darkness. The only thing that made any sense to me in those early days was reading the Bible or hearing the Word of God spoken. I could understand the things of the Spirit, but wasn't functioning well on the natural plane that still seemed to be shrouded in fantasy. How my daughters survived is a mystery! One brother said I must have had several angel squadrons assigned to our little family.

God's searchlight had been turned on, revealing how much I needed to be restored. That night I left the meeting glowing with fresh fire and a new inner strength, and began a new walk with God.

Aimee celebrating Easter on Partington Ridge

Chapter Thirteen

Jesus Comes to Nepenthe

It was well known that I was an airhead, still really "out there," and many brethren were praying for my healing. For example, I bought a car even though I had no idea how to drive. When Eileen tried to teach me it became very evident to her that my mind wasn't healed enough. Ruth was less nervous and offered to give me a lesson on the road behind Deetjen's Big Sur Inn. But my reactions were too fast on the gas and much too slow on the brake. So, once again others had to drive me here and there, and the classic 1967 VW hatchback I had bought from Selig Morgenrath, Helen's ex-husband, became a great blessing for many in our fellowship.

With a confidence I had never known before, I started praying aloud in tongues as I walked up and down the ridge near my garden. I understood then that the gift of a heavenly language was for worship to the Lord and for a weapon against Satan. As I spoke those strange words to God, I felt such a powerful resistance mounting up against the enemy of my soul. I was pushing back now, and learning spiritual warfare! Of course the attacks still came, but less often, until they finally stopped altogether. Since those prayers that night for my deliverance, the fresh oil of the Holy Spirit had been poured into my soul, and a new fire had been ignited. I began to use scripture as I prayed out loud, and learned that there was no power on earth, or in the air (*Satan is called the "prince and power of the air"*) that could overcome the truth inherent in the spoken Word of God.

Somehow I got a job working as Nepenthe's "family cook" in Lolly's kitchen, preparing meals for all the employees when Faye was no longer able to do it. She coached me, and Annie, Bill's niece, may have put in a good word for me. I was thrilled to be there again, but as a very different person this time. I felt at home, yet Nepenthe had become a very different turf. I was delighted to discover that many new Christians worked there. We often met around the kitchen table after I had made lunch, and shared what God was doing among us. The windows of heaven had opened upon Nepenthe. It seemed as though everything then was touched by the miraculous, and I was delighted to earn my own way again, and get off the welfare dole.

In fact, we had begun meeting at Kim and John's house down below the main cabin. Kim was Lolly's youngest daughter and the mother of two beautiful children, Cappy and Nani, born from a previous relationship. She and John were very much in love with each other and with God, and decided they wanted to be married. Bro. Abbott performed the ceremony on the Phoenix Balcony, and Lolly made a very special wedding cake from a family recipe. Kim was very simply dressed in a long white cotton dress she had borrowed from Lois DeFord, and wore a crown of flowers with ribbons trailing down her long hair. She was naturally very beautiful, and radiated the joy of Jesus and her new found faith. John wore an embroidered white Indian shirt, white trousers, and sandals. He sported a trimmed beard and looked so elegant. It was quite an event for the Nepenthe family, and for our little band of Christians. Lolly and others from the Fassett family seemed delighted with the match. John's southern charm had successfully disarmed all their misgivings about these new Christians.

Our meetings took on a new flavor as we gathered in front of the little house John and Kim called home, located near a small garden on Nepenthe's property. Sis. Abbott came to be with us on Sundays, and her preaching was the highlight of the week. She dressed in long skirts to fit in with her hippie children, and her English accent and perfect enunciation made everything she said so delightful to us. She embraced everyone as they came in, and just loved on us. Her speaking voice was very dramatic, accompanied by graceful gestures, and we all thought she could easily have had her own Christian television program. The very fact of living in this gorgeous landscape seemed to color all our habitats with the mystique of an old Hollywood film set.

And indeed, Hollywood had invaded this little corner of the world and projected its star power onto the Big Sur collective psyche. Ever since the days of *The Sandpiper*, a romantic film starring Elizabeth Taylor and Richard Burton (then lovers on film and in real life) Big Sur had been subtly transformed into a kind of *glass menagerie* by its magic wand. The film's success had brought worldwide attention to Nepenthe's Restaurant and Big Sur, using the double allure of its own natural beauty and the sheer glamour of these star-crossed lovers. Big Sur eventually became an even more powerful magnet drawing the rich and the famous. Somehow we were all subtly aware of being watched by those who saw us as interesting characters from another world they wanted to believe was real, especially in the days when the hippie culture took center stage at Nepenthe.

Though another restaurant, called Ventana, had opened its doors with great fanfare, and offered tourists elegant gourmet food, lodging, and a lovely vista, Lolly certainly had not been troubled by the appearance of a rival. And she needn't have been. Nepenthe remained, and still remains, the iconic focal point of natural beauty and Big Sur society. It held a magic and charm that simply could never be duplicated, and its history had been deeply rooted in local legend and native mythology. And so a local custom practiced there inadvertently drew a line in the sand for me while I was still working as a cook. Lolly always threw "astrology birthday" parties every month to cover all the signs in the zodiac. It was my turn to bake a cake for one, and I had a crisis of conscience because I no longer believed in the significance of astrological signs. I had to go and tell Lolly that I couldn't do it, knowing it might cost me my job. I think she had to call Faye back to make the cake, and was very upset with me, and I heard her mutter the word *mutiny* under her breath.

Lolly was a woman very dear to me, one who had befriended Aimée and me at the lowest point in our lives. I must have disappointed her and I felt so bad, not wanting to betray our friendship. But Lolly had indeed become the captain of this ship, overseeing the staff and all the logistics. Her husband Bill had long ago abdicated his post at the wheel, and lived away in Carmel. He was involved with a woman named Alice, a talented English designer who had taken over the Phoenix dress shop at Bill's insistence (*she would also give him another child*). Lolly had survived this affair by becoming stronger in her role at Nepenthe. Eventually she let me go, and other cooks came on the scene, eager to be part of the family there.

One incident in particular stands out from those meeting days near Nepenthe's garden. Sis. Abbott came loaded with lovely white gift boxes tied with ribbon, and gave each of the ladies one. We were all startled to see what was inside, a very delicate English bone China teacup! We sat in stunned silence before anyone could speak. These gifts had come down to us from the storybook world of long ago. Our idea of making a cup of tea was crushing leaves of yerba buena and then stuffing them into a metal teapot which we left sitting on the woodstove, and pouring the tea into a mason jar, or a cracked mug. I looked at my very own cup for a long time with tears in my eyes, and wondered how I could bring this delicate beauty into my dusty little cabin. We were all laughing at the cultural incongruity of it all, but were very touched by her desire to bless us. Mine probably stayed in its box as a keepsake for a long time. I was afraid to actually handle it for fear of breaking it, and never felt worthy enough to drink from it.

Sis. Abbott had often brought us clothes and underwear she collected from her church lady friends. She must have intrigued them with descriptions of our lack of material things, our lack of clothing, and especially underclothing. After she left, we would laugh at the selection of old-fashioned panties and slips, knowing we could never wear them. In her eyes we were similar to the African natives she and her husband had preached among. Though we weren't swinging from the trees, we still seemed primitive enough to their proper English eyes. She and her husband had worked in the jungles of West Africa, and brought the Gospel message to villages that had never seen white people. So, our lifestyle seemed oddly familiar to them. She often joined us for a swim in the Big Sur River, and we all dressed as well as we could for the occasion. All I could muster up was a short black leotard I had left from Helen's dance classes. The older children were delighted to catch crawdads, and the toddlers played on the sandy shore. Some of the ladies preferred to crochet or knit, while enjoying the summer sun.

Whenever we met for a Bible study in someone's home, Bro. Abbott learned to accept the tumult of our children nursing, crawling, playing and sitting in with us, as well as the ladies doing handiwork, while he shared his message. We knew this went against his English etiquette and ministry protocol. We definitely wouldn't fit within the church world he knew, and in a sense, he never wanted us to become "churchy," and he tried not to quench our spirit of liberty. Instead, he saw us as spiritual trophies of an authentic Christian community growing up in the midst of a distinctly foreign culture, very far removed from the deadness of church formalities, and he must have bragged about us often to fellow pastors in town. Of course, the Abbotts always brought any visiting ministers to lunch at Nepenthe, the spectacular gathering place for anyone coming to Big Sur. They would regale them with incredible stories about us, punctuated by the dramatic backdrop of an immense blue sky above and the roaring ocean beneath them, pounding against the steep rocky coastland. These visitors must have been so impressed to hear about the authentic New Testament church God was building in this incredible place. Don and Florence, who had no children of their own, exulted in us like proud parents, and took their share of the glory for our changed lives.

Chapter Fourteen

The Vine Grows Over the Wall

Carefully following the New Testament pattern laid down by the apostle Paul, Bro. Abbott appointed Tom, Ruth, and Bob DeFord as elders, or overseers, of our growing flock. They were responsible to guide us in our walk with God, and to pray for us when we slipped into error or sin. As an example, I once shared with Tom's wife, Sue, that I still enjoyed a glass of my prized Spanish sherry at night. She looked concerned, and asked if I thought this was pleasing to the Lord. Well, I hadn't thought it was wrong, but hadn't asked God about it either. When I did pray about it, I felt sure that He was asking me to pour it out as a love offering to Him, and to be filled only with His Spirit. Since my family had had a problem with alcohol, it seemed best then that I refrain completely, which I did from that time onward. Ceremoniously taking the half-full bottle outside the cabin, I poured the remaining wine onto the ground, in a very biblical gesture, and felt very spiritual indeed.

Another casual conversation with Sue proved to be a personal anathema. She smilingly said there would be no wild dancing anymore on Nepenthe's terrace for me! I almost choked with despair because her words seemed so hard to swallow. I knew that we were all being trained to "avoid the very appearance of evil," and the rhythms of rock and roll did bring out the sensual exhibitionist in me. Dancing had always been part of my adult life, and the thought of never enjoying it again was almost too hard to bear. And yet—for Jesus—I was willing to forego this delicious freedom, and not allow myself to be an occasion of sinful thought to anyone else.

But I could comfort myself with another minor victory in my life. The Holy Spirit had spoken directly to me that smoking was not honoring my body as His temple, causing me to fall prostrate before Him. I began in earnest then to quit altogether. After many months of constant struggle with heavy cigarette addiction, I could congratulate myself that I had been able to reduce my smoking to one cigarette a day! I had even stopped buying cigarettes altogether and would—ever so self-righteously—ask a friend or a neighbor for a cigarette as my reward each evening before bedtime. Then a day came when my request turned it all around.

Ruth's brother George was staying with her at the time, and came up to visit our little family, and talk with some of the brethren who were staying with us. Because he was still a smoker, I looked to him for my "reward" that day. When I asked him, "Can I have a cigarette?" he smiled politely and said, "No." His answer sent me into a tailspin, but I knew God's Spirit had prompted it. I turned to walk back to the cabin, embarrassed and shaken. Inside, I fell to my knees, and let the waves of withdrawal roll over me. From that moment on, I continued to say no until the habit died and I was free. Amazingly, it took a real friend refusing to give me a crutch that evening that enabled me to walk in victory for the rest of my life.

Meanwhile, our fellowship was slowly being cross-fertilized with other Pentecostal churches whenever we visited the Salinas brethren. It must have a shock for them to have this scraggly, wild-looking bunch of country bumpkins come strolling down the aisle, and promptly sit on the floor in front, yoga style, hungry to be fed spiritual food. It was the first time we ever saw Bro. Abbott preach a sermon in normal Pentecostal style. He would jump and up down behind the pulpit, or run down the aisle shouting like a house was on fire! Then the people would shout "Hallelujah" and "Amen" back at him, and bang their tambourines with gusto. It both scared and delighted us to hear him, and also to see some ladies dance around the church clearly oblivious of our presence. Soon the whole church would be dancing, and we happily joined them.

After the initial fear of being irreverent, I grew to love the kind of liberty they enjoyed and thought I could never again be satisfied with the quiet worship style of Catholics. This congregation was so involved in their vocal response that I never again wanted to be part of a passive audience, or be an onlooker warming the pew, waiting to be fed or entertained. At times we would be invited to sing some of the songs the Lord had given us, and bless the churches with our musical gifts. Bro. Abbott would also arrange outdoor concerts for us as a way of sharing God's message of forgiveness, and many people came to know Jesus through this outpouring of homespun music and real-life testimonies.

We also used to visit a black "Bapticostal" church in Seaside, where some of our members actually sang in the choir, and all of us were equally astonished by the fervency this congregation exhibited in worship. One never knew when a brother or sister would be so touched by the Spirit they would suddenly disappear under the pew, or fall down on some unsuspecting choir member. It was all a part of God's mysterious workings among one of his families on earth. Dorcas, Kim's older sister, became a Christian later on, and eventually joined a similar church in Seaside where she served the Lord for many years. Of course I couldn't help but think of my mother walking into such a church, and running out in fear of her life.

We were once invited by Glen Harlan, who came from one of the early pioneer Big Sur families, to attend a Sunday meeting at a small country church. It looked like a real "chapel in the wildwood" if ever there was one, and belonged to some Seventh Day Adventists near Lucia, on the South Coast. The message was centered on Jesus' sacrifice on the cross, and we left there delighted to have found another native Big Sur band of Christians. Bro. Abbott, though, was not too happy with our discovery and our glowing reports. He informed us about the theology that had come from their teacher named Ellen White, whom some Christians considered a false prophetess. Then we began to notice that whenever Glen came to our meetings all he wanted was to expound his doctrine rather than participate in our worship, so our relationship with him withered.

Many others who lived in Big Sur flowed in and out of our lives, drawn by the love we offered, the music we sang, and the food we shared. I fondly remember Larry and Judy Share, a beautiful Jewish couple, and their children, Kevin and Vanessa. They became good friends with Tom and Sue soon after they came to live in Big Sur. We enjoyed seeing how they raised their beautiful family and welcomed them to join in activities, which they did for quite awhile. A French Catholic couple named Eric and Therese loved to join in our outdoor worship services, and blessed our lives for a season.

Our meetings were soon to change course yet again. We had enjoyed meeting in the quiet simplicity of Tom and Sue's cabin for a year or so, and then our gatherings outside in the garden with many from Nepenthe at John and Kim's house. But we were growing too large in number and need, so we decided to rent the Grange Hall for a potluck and Bible study that could include our Salinas brethren who frequently came to visit us. The Abbotts wanted us to share a fellowship meal, exchange testimonies about what God was doing in our lives, and worship together. At that point they wanted our little church body to continue growing in its native land of Big Sur. Our Grange Hall meetings created a cultural collision that had a major impact on our Big Sur family and those from Salinas. We all had come from very different backgrounds and lifestyles. Some of those from Salinas had been heroin addicts, or gang bangers and prostitutes; and some of us from Big Sur were tripped-out hippies and New Age spiritual seekers. Our commonality was based only in the fact that we were all sinners who needed a Savior.

The brethren from Salinas often brought day-old donuts to our dwellings and our meetings, thinking they were blessing our sugar-starved souls. They liked to share comfort food like fried chicken, mashed potatoes, and casseroles. We would bring a healthy variety of fresh garden vegetables, homemade soups or salads, rice, and beans. Some of their ladies wore makeup, fancy clothes, fixed their hair nicely, and painted their toenails. Sitting next to them, we were indeed a mixture of longhairs, oddballs, and plain-janes, and all a little on the dusty side. Some of us had lived in greenhouses, or even inside tree trunks, had run naked through the woods, grown our own vegetables (as well as our own marijuana), baked our own bread, cut our own firewood, raised goats and chickens, and took our baths in the river. At first we secretly complained about their food, and planned to teach them the virtues of good eating. Because we were convinced that Jesus was coming back soon, many of us gradually forgot our health-food values and let the sugar have its way. But we aslo learned not to be so critical of their lifestyle, to enjoy our time with them, and to share the growing excitement over our baptisms, the first of many to come—and many wedding ceremonies. Bro. Abbott officiated at the marriages of Hal and Barbara Rightmyer, Stan and Diana Herrin, and Wes and Barbara Baker. They were all performed in a profoundly beautiful but simple country setting, with no frills and no pomp, but sprinkled with plenty of brotherly love.

And so, Aimée, age eight, and I, age thirty-five, came together with Ruth, Rita, Tom and Sue, John and Kim, Lois and Bob DeFord, for the first Big Sur baptism. Many others had gathered in Pfeiffer State Park to watch as Bro. Abbott immersed us in the Big Sur River that was still very cold that spring. This was a huge step for us in obedience to Jesus' command to be baptized. We were declaring to Big Sur and beyond that we were not ashamed to be numbered among His followers. It was, in effect, a token of our spiritual resurrection from sin's dark hold. We all felt inwardly cleansed, and shivered with delight as we stepped out of the water, eagerly looking forward to a future of more new beginnings. The memory of all those happy faces shining with tears of joy, as we praised God and cheered one another on, still glows brightly as one of the happiest days of my life. Since then, attending any baptismal service brings joyous tears of remembrance to my eyes.

The Abbotts began to spend more personal time with us. It was mostly delightful but also a little intimidating. I remember once when Sis. Abbott was visiting us in our little cabin that she almost went over the cliff as she drove away. The wheels of her big yellow Ford sedan were only half on the road, and the other two spun in the air. We sent for help, and stared in wonder at what must have been angels holding up the car, preventing it from rolling over the embankment. Earlier that day she had commented that I lived like a queen in such a beautiful setting, but without a "king" to share our little kingdom. I could give her no reason, except that I needed to be healed of a broken heart and mind. Big Sur seemed to foster an almost matriarchal culture due to the very independent breed of woman it produced, and I was fast becoming one of them. After all, my favorite scripture then was "...there is neither male nor female, for you are all one in Christ." (Gal. 3:28)

Eventually the Abbotts parked their little trailer in Big Sur so that Sis. Abbott could be available if any of us wanted private counsel. She even stayed in an A-frame house on our ridge for a season, in an effort to bond with us. Perhaps because of the differences between her tightly knit English culture and our loosely knit American culture (or our present immaturity), we couldn't fully embrace her. She seemed to be in a spiritual class all by herself, and certainly one to which we could ever hope to attain. I remember sitting with her on a rock near the Grange on a Sunday, when she told me I was so much like her. It shocked me to the core, and begged the questions: *Do I really want to be like her? Does she have any idea what I have done, or what darkness I came from?* It would take the next twenty years for me to fully answer those questions.

Although it was often a very frightening and humiliating experience, I was very grateful that Sis. Abbott prayed to deliver me from evil spirits that still lingered around me and in my soul. After our early cabin meeting days, she would look deep into my eyes and say, "Are there any more in there?" I learned to trust her discernment in this realm, until I could discern the presence of evil spirits myself, and was able to participate in someone else's spiritual deliverance. What once had been a curse on my life became a source of blessing for others. However, her greatest spiritual gift became evident whenever we gathered together for group prayer. She taught us to pray using scripture as our foundation, and with passion, intensity, and great liberty. For many years I thought we had to shout our prayers like she did in order to be heard, but gradually learned that God is not deaf, and bends down to hear the tiniest whisper of a prayer.

During that time, I had a very distinct impression that I needed to share this message of salvation with Jeff, still legally my husband, who was living on top of Partington Ridge, still with the young girl named Peaches. It was very hard on me emotionally, but I obeyed the Spirit of God, and a brother, Bob DeFord, agreed to accompany me. We walked up the road until we saw Peaches standing near a tent where Jeff sat naked in a yoga pose. She seemed shy and a little embarrassed when I told her who I was, and why I had come. Bob stood silently beside me. Jeff just smiled as I spoke to them about what Jesus had done for me, and then I invited them to one of our meetings. I left feeling self-righteous and satisfied that I had done my duty.

To my surprise and chagrin, they both came the next Sunday and caused quite a stir among the brethren. Sis. Abbott greeted Jeff, not knowing who he was, and immediately laid hands on his head, having to stand on a chair because he was so tall. He fell down under the power of the Holy Spirit and she continued to pray over him. I watched as Peaches bowed her head and let some tears fall on her trembling lips. When he returned to his senses, he got up from the floor and soon left after he had spoken with some people he knew. I just hid from sight in a state of shock and inner turmoil. *What could this mean? What would happen if Jeff became a Christian? What did it mean for our relationship, or for his girlfriend?*

It created yet another kind of spiritual dilemma for me, as I had been attracted to a brother named Steve, and wondered if God was going to bless me with a Christian husband and father for my children. Steve and I used to meet in the mornings for prayer near Nepenthe's garden while I was cooking meals in Lolly's kitchen. I watched him play baseball with the brothers and he seemed so normal compared to the men I had known in the past. By then I was longing for some semblance of normality. When Jeff didn't show up again at the Grange I breathed a sigh of relief mixed with pangs of guilt. He had no intention of changing his lifestyle, or his drug habits. I learned later that Peaches had been raised a Christian and had taken him to her church in Palo Alto, where God's Spirit touched him again and again. *Years later she actually called me to repent for her dalliance with Jeff. We cannot say nor see who belongs to God and who doesn't, because only God really knows who His children are. It is one of the great mysteries of our faith. I have prayed for Jeff, and left him in God's hands.*

Soon after that I made a phone call to Sis. Abbott for guidance, and asked the big question of whether I should divorce Jeff or not. She shared that I was called to peace and not confusion. She assured me that God's Spirit would lead me. I felt released from any guilt and went to the library asking for the legal papers I needed to start the process. Soon Jeff was served with the papers somewhere, and I knew he would not contest the divorce. He didn't. I didn't want any alimony, and formally granted him the visitation rights he would never request or ever use. It took me less than a year to close that chapter of my life, and I felt empowered by the fact I had completed the whole legal matter by myself, and for free. But the reality that I had been divorced from a husband who had been seen very much alive by all, cast a long shadow over my relationship with Steve. And because God had other plans, and cared for both of us so much, He would soon step into our lives in a startling way.

Our Fellowship had reached a certain level of spiritual maturity, and we had all grown very close in heart and mind. A handsome long-haired young man named James Laney joined us soon after he left a commune. Ruth was mentoring him and noted his ability to preach. He soon became one of the elders. As a spiritual family, we abounded in musical and spiritual gifts, and were eager to help one another with our needs, willing to share all we had and learning to hear the voice of the Spirit. We prayed for anyone who was open to God and who had expressed a need. Once I was prompted to seek out an older woman, also named Ruth, someone I knew only slightly, who had cancer. She had worked as a waitress at Nepenthe for many years and was standing at the bar as Annie and I approached, to tell her why we had come. Without any hesitation we laid hands upon her, and prayed for God to heal her. It seemed that we had walked there in a cloud of glory, and were not conscious of anyone except God. After we left, we heard later that God had touched her for a season with Divine health.

Chapter Fifteen

Exiles in Exodus

During that time, Bro. Abbott met a man who changed his life and then, all of ours. His name was R. Edward Miller, a missionary to Argentina during the 50s, who had seen a remarkable move of God's Spirit. He and his family still lived in Mar del Plata as pastors to the church and Bible Institute there, but had come to the States to minister at summer camp meetings at various churches, sharing about the unusual supernatural manifestations of God their ministry had experienced. Bro. Miller had spent six months in a prayer closet seeking God for Argentina before he saw hearts become more open to the message of Jesus. Then there was an angelic visitation to children in an orphanage nearby, during which there were visions of heaven and miracles of healing. From that point on, he said, they lived under *an open heaven.* What had once been supernatural and rarely seen became natural and more frequent, and the country of Argentina was ushered into a several decades-long spiritual revival. This slightly older, gentle white-haired minister became Bro. Abbott's mentor for a very short period of time, and was possibly the only person other than Dave Wilkerson that Bro. Abbott had ever allowed to exert a certain kind of influence or spiritual authority over him. And Bob Miller, Bro. Miller's son, was to exert another kind of spiritual influence on our fellowship both in Big Sur and Salinas for a season as well.

Bro. Abbott was excited to tell the Millers about what was happening in Big Sur, especially with our group of hippies, and asked Edward Miller to come and help us prepare our first camp meeting. It was to take place in Pfeiffer State Park and would become the focal point for different ministries to come together in the unity of prayer and fellowship. A small group of new Christians in Carmel Valley and nearby Palo Colorado canyon had heard about us, and were invited to come. Others, from an independent group in Las Vegas, which called itself "Maranatha," also joined us.

None of us had any idea then what camp meetings were, nor any inkling that these annual meetings would become an integral part of our spiritual lives. The Methodist tradition, later adopted by Pentecostals, was intended as a spiritual retreat for the whole church and for an occasion to baptize all the newer members.

We looked forward to this special time together, and Steve and I thought it might be a good time for a wedding also. What we didn't know then was that different brethren had expressed concern over our relationship to the Abbotts. These brethren had sensed Steve's uneasiness and realized that I was blithely bouncing along unaware that something wasn't quite right. As we met with them on the first evening of that camp meeting, they asked Steve if he was ready for commitment, and he said no. That burst any bubble I had about marrying him, so we decided to call off the wedding. It was a very painful awakening for both of us. God had stepped into our lives and rearranged our plans according to His plan. Unfortunately, the girls had to bear the brunt of my disappointment, as I explained why marriage wasn't God's will for me at that time.

Steve would later ask Annie to be his wife, and I remember that she had once shared with me that God had revealed to her that she and Steve would be married. That first camp meeting had been ordained to set me free to wait for the partner that God had for me. But that's another story.

Some other changes took place during camp meeting. Bro. Miller had introduced us to a deeper realm of worship. As a group, we had learned how to praise the Lord in the "outer courts," but now we all entered into a new place of spiritual intimacy with God that he called the "Holy of Holies." It reminded me of our times in Carmel with the Uphams, when we all sang together in the Spirit using our new spiritual language, and how it had created unearthly harmonies. I remember the ecstasy I felt as we joined hands and danced in a circle that first night at camp meeting! "Hope deferred makes the heart sick," but the oil of joy was poured over me as I danced and sang in the Spirit with my brethren. God lifted me up to a place of safety under His wings, where there was peace and trust. His hand had reached down once again to touch my life, and change my destiny.

Bro. Miller had been captivated by the joyful spontaneity and simple way of life we lived as Christians there. But he became concerned as he gradually realized how much a part of the Big Sur culture we really were. His son Bob had been sharing with the elders about the group's rebellious attitude toward any form of authority and toward normal society in general. After praying with the Abbotts one evening, Bro. Ed Miller proposed that our group should leave Big Sur, because we weren't strong enough yet to resist the dark powers there, especially the spirit of rebellion. He sensed we were still too immature in our knowledge of God and His ways. Then he dared to ask if Bro. Abbott would be willing to incorporate us into the Salinas fellowship, and compared him to Moses, leading God's people out of Egypt. At first, Bro. Abbott was simply too overwhelmed by this suggestion, and couldn't agree. He was sure that God had wanted a local Body of Christ to stay planted there in Big Sur. The thought of pulling us up by the roots came against all that he had envisioned for us becoming: a lighthouse, a city on a hill, and a refuge for this lost generation of spiritual seekers.

When he finally unloaded this bombshell on the group, there were two very opposite reactions. Most of the younger members were delighted to leave, and start a new life elsewhere. Some of the older members, especially Tom and Sue, Ruth, Rita, Kim and John, were unwilling to make the move. For them it was more than just pulling up stakes. They were deeply rooted in the community, and had enjoyed a long history there. Tom and Sue lived on an enviable piece of property into which they had invested time and money. Kim and John were part of the Nepenthe family dynasty that had even deeper historical ties to Big Sur. It just seemed unthinkable for them to leave. Bob and Lois had already moved into town, because Bob didn't agree with Bro. Abbott's ministry any longer, or with the direction the Fellowship was taking.

Personally I was conflicted. Part of me was not yet ready to exit the land of my second birth. In general, we were still welcome in the community, and many people were still very pleased with us. At times there were conflicts and misunderstandings. I remember the sculptor Buzz Brown lampooning us as a group by building what he called *Noah's Ark* in front of the River Inn, the local bar. He had heard about a book we were reading, called *The Late, Great Planet Earth,* which talked about an "end times," and this was his way of mocking us as a people. The truth was that we all truly believed then that Jesus was coming back soon, even immediately, and we wanted to be ready. I had actually thought of going to Israel to wait for Him at the foot of Mt. Olivet, the exact place of His return.

Big Sur had been my home for almost seven years, and the place of my redemption. It had been a type of Eden for so many of us. We had once believed that we were "stardust and golden," and thought we had gotten "back to the garden," as Joni Mitchell's song told us. Yet, just as our first parents had experienced, was God now casting us out? Had we tasted the forbidden fruit, the knowledge of good and evil? I knew my eyes had been opened, and that I was naked. I also knew I now lived in another realm, God's Kingdom of Light, yet could not comprehend the reality of what it would mean to leave this enchanted earthly paradise.

After the first group of young ones had gone, those that had not left still met together, feeling left behind, and a little desolate. We questioned the breakup of our fellowship, and prayed about what we should do. Bro. Abbott would visit and let us know that everyone had been well received and were adapting to the change, that the Salinas brethren had ecstatically embraced them. The enlarged fellowship had rented a room above a bank in Salinas, where he and Bro. Miller held meetings. Bro. Abbott said they were more powerful than anything he had ever known before.

A part of me was so hungry to experience what he described, but I was told to wait because I still needed so much emotional healing. Slowly more of our group began to leave for Salinas. Those that remained were deeply counting the cost of leaving one of the most beautiful places on earth, one they had been privileged to call home. It was a great sacrifice that weighed heavily on everyone: to exchange an idyllic way of life, wonderful jobs, close friends and family, for a place that seemed so mundane and nondescript. Leaving all that was held dear and precious, all that they valued in life, and becoming a foreigner, a stranger in a strange land, required a lot of prayer and fasting. It wasn't something to be done lightly.

I had moved down from the ridge into a small cabin on Amelia Newell's property behind Deetjen's Inn, sold my VW for a good price since I still wasn't able to drive it, and stocked up on groceries. The girls and I liked being so close to the Inn, and enjoyed bowls of their delicious soup now and then. Aimée missed all her friends, having only little Lucy for a playmate, but they became very close during our brief exile. She had blossomed both physically and spiritually. Once as we walked on one of the trails that took us over the ridges, I heard an anointing come upon her voice as she sang softly to the Lord. I was so thankful that she could grow up safely now, and in such purity. Lucia too had become such a blessing to the fellowship; her bright personality and smile opened many a fearful heart. Though she was only 5 years old, it was hard to resist her manner of connecting with the lonely ones who hung around the edges of our fellowship. Because she spoke and interacted with people like a miniature adult, and was so petite, we lovingly called her "Midge."

Meanwhile, our spiritual family slowly exited Big Sur, causing quite a few tremors of misunderstanding, emotional pain, and resentment. There were those in Big Sur who were convinced that a South African cult leader had taken control of us, and had beguiled us into giving up family and friends, houses, and land. Admittedly, it was hard to understand, and harder to explain that we felt God was leading us out. We were told that most of the brethren there in Salinas were single and much younger, and that they lived together in large houses. I was a single mother with two children; there was just no place to put us then. Finally, only we three remained in Big Sur.

The months of separation were beginning to cause doubts about whether or not we would ever leave. Then one evening, just as Lucy was recovering from a very high fever and cough, Amelia burst through the door and abruptly said, "You must leave now!" She gave no reason for her decision to throw us out. Our rent was paid on time, we were quiet as church mice, but her face was hard-set in anger and contempt. I found myself shaking with fear, engulfed in another fresh wave of abandonment. The girls started crying when I couldn't give them an answer for the lingering question, "Why, what have we done?" There was nothing I could do but reach out for help from Salinas, so I called Bro. Abbott to explain our predicament. He said not to worry, that Bro. George Iman would come immediately and pick us up! I told the girls, and we all laughed for joy. We would soon be reunited with all our friends, and no longer feel like displaced persons marooned on a distant island.

When Bro. George showed up, he helped put our few belongings in his black pickup. He was like a son to Bro. Abbott, and was one of the elders in Salinas. His ruddy face, joyful laugh and gentle smile put us at ease. The girls piled into the back of the truck, and huddled under some blankets, eager to begin a new chapter in our lives. Bro. George smiled as he started the engine. Then I turned to him and said something neither one of us was prepared to hear: "You're not going to tame me"! He gasped aloud, shook his head in disbelief, and then laughed. We were both startled by the fierceness of my words, but my mouth spoke what was hidden in my heart. We remained politely silent for the rest of the journey, listening to Christian songs on the radio.

End of Book One

Big Sur Fellowship meeting at the Grange

Cestimonies from the Jesus Revolution

Annie Johnson Campbell

I was raised in Laguna Beach, California, graduating from high school in 1969. We never attended church, except a Catholic church one Christmas Eve, and we all hated it. But one day my mother and I were walking to the library, as we often did, and we saw a manger scene at the front of the building. I asked her what it was, as I never remembered seeing one before. I didn't know then she was an avowed atheist, yet she openly explained the Christmas story to me. As I lay in bed that night and thought of Jesus and Mary, I remember feeling safe, for the first time, and fell asleep peacefully. Many other nights I would hear strange noises outside, or in the walls, and once awoke to find people around my bed, talking to me. I don't think it was a dream, but evil spirits tormenting me. I often made the perilous trip through the house in the middle of the night to my parents' bedroom, because I was so scared.

When I was 17, my mother gave me a box of occult books that had belonged to my grandmother. I looked through them with only mild curiosity but was powerfully gripped by their contents. Unknowingly I had opened a Pandora's box and was soon reading palms, doing astrology charts, and reading tarot cards. It seemed like "magic" that I learned so quickly. I now believe there were spirits attached to these things. The other thing that happened was a group of Christian college students came to my high school and gave their testimonies and told us to ask Jesus to come into our hearts. So obediently, after school, I did just that. Apparently nothing happened, as far as I could tell, so I continued merrily down my personal path to hell. After all, I was living in the 60s, and in a California beach town. My idyllic life as a beach bum/body surfer/volleyball player was soon left behind in a haze of drugs, sex, and the occult. Drugs were the doorway into all of these. As a result, I became isolated, depressed, introverted, unmotivated, confused, and above all, searching for answers.

One turning point came in San Diego when I was invited to attend a séance of sorts. My friends had called it only, "Dan's Class," so it sounded innocent enough. There were about 40 people sitting on chairs in a big circle with 4 people at a table in the center. The table would tap out people's names and that person would be "blessed" with some sort of visitation or revelation. Well sure enough "it" tapped out my name. What I experienced was somehow intolerable to me, and I remember leaping out of my chair shouting, "Stop! I don't like this!" and ran out of the building never to return!

Another turning point was when a dear friend died of a heroin overdose. What a moment of light came into my darkness! I knew, the moment I heard, why I had believed in the occult and reincarnation. I knew as surely as I knew my name that I was afraid to die and meet God. Just a few months before then she and I had been together, talking about the Jesus Freaks and their message. We agreed they were probably right, but that we were not ready for it. But now she was dead at age 20.

Another significant moment in my journey to God happened when I was waiting for a bus in San Diego. A funky hippie girl sat down next to me and started telling me about Jesus. She asked if I knew about the Gospel. "Oh yes," I said, "lots of my friends are Christians." Her response? "Have they told you that you're going to Hell?" Then she stood up and walked away! Her words had pierced me to my core, like a bolt of lightning. TRUTH! I knew, for the first time that what she said was true.

During the very difficult last year I attended San Diego State, the year my friend died, there was a song on the radio by Judy Collins: "Open the door and come on in, I'm so glad to see you my friends, you're all like rainbows coming around the bend. And when I see you happy, well it sets my heart free. I want to be as good a friend to you as you are to me." It was called "Song For Judith." Every time I heard it tears came to my eyes, and I longed for a family, a deep longing to belong. The song became my theme and my dream. I felt so isolated from everyone and everything. Sin and the devil have a way of doing just that. My search was taking me further downward into darkness, and I knew it.

All of this culminated in my dropping out of college in May of 1972 and moving to Big Sur, California, where my Uncle Bill and Aunt Lolly had a famous restaurant called Nepenthe. I knew I could get a job and living quarters there. I was determined to turn over a new leaf—mainly I wanted to stop the drugs and promiscuity. Those were my goals but it was shocking to find out that I could not do it. I had always been able to do whatever I set my mind to, no problem! But suddenly I seemed to have a ball and chain around my ankle, with no will of my own. I had really hit a brick wall and come to a dead end.

Now let me back up about a hundred years here and go to Chattanooga, Tennessee, to meet my great-grandfather, Thomas Hooke McCallie. He was a godly man of prayer, who had often prayed for "the generations yet to come." And here I was, one of his descendants, living and working at a restaurant built and owned by one of his descendants, my uncle Bill. And this was also the place in Big Sur where God had chosen to mightily pour out His Spirit! It was a real hub of activity then, and many people who worked there turned their hearts to the Lord in the early 70s. I was one of them. After I'd been there a few months, I met "The Christians," as everyone called them, and I was inexplicably drawn to them, like a moth to a flame. It was all way beyond my control. Where they were, I wanted to be. Where they went, I wanted to go, following them around like a lost puppy. This all came to a climax at a birthday party on Pfeiffer Ridge in Big Sur. I had to leave because I simply could not stay away from these Christians! As I drove down the mountain, tears spilled down my cheeks and for the first time in my life I cried out to God: "Oh God! What is happening to me! I feel like I am losing my mind!" I heard a voice, suddenly, from nowhere, saying clearly, "I want you to give me your mind." I was so shocked I laughed out loud! I went from crying in anguish to laughter and chuckles all the way home. I could not get over it. It so obviously did not come from me, that idea would never have come from me! It had to be from God, and how could He possibly ask that of me?

I thought I'd better start reading the Bible, and see what was in there. My only acquaintance with the Book of Books was through reading *Autobiography of a Yogi* a few years earlier. Whenever the author quoted Jesus I found His words powerful and true! I had looked just about everywhere to find truth, except Jesus. Christianity seemed to be something for weak, needy, "un-evolved" individuals. My mind viewed Jesus and His stories to be no more than fairytales. But in my heart, I felt differently. I could call them fairytales all I wanted, but anytime someone else said that, I knew they were wrong.

So I began to read the Bible in my little room at Nepenthe. All I did for two weeks in my spare time was to read the Bible. I turned here, I turned there, but it all seemed to say the same thing: "Come out from among them and be separate and I will receive you and be a Father to you and you shall be my child." God was supernaturally pointing me to this Scripture over and over until, lo and behold, I came to Him. I don't know how it happened, but I know I didn't want to go to the Halloween party at Nepenthe. It somehow felt wrong. So I didn't. Instead I went to their "church" that Sunday, which was at my cousin Kim's house just down the road. I was welcomed by the brethren and the pastor's wife with open arms as a sister in the Lord, only because God must have shown them I belonged to Him now. That night at a Christian school in Watsonville, I was baptized into His Holy Spirit. There seemed to be a mighty choir all around me, praising God, and I suspect there truly was. Heaven rejoices when a lost lamb comes home. And boy, was I ever home. I had never in my life experienced joy, peace, love, abounding and out-flowing like I experienced in those beginning of days. I didn't even know such a thing existed. In all my occult readings, I had never been prepared for a joyous union with God. It was always something that seemed more like a coma, more like a living death, to be rid of the pains of Life. But this! This was an ecstasy in which I lived and moved and had my being, waking or sleeping. I had met God and He was AWESOME! I felt a huge crushing burden had been lifted off my back. He had forgiven my sins, which were many.

That was more than 40 years ago in Big Sur. Since that time I have read the Bible almost daily and prayed to God about almost everything. I have come to believe with certainty that He is real, that He is exactly who He says He is in His Word, that He answers prayer, and that He longs for us to wait for Him, for His ways and His answers, as a child waits on their Father. I have come to know that He is good and kind and just, and not willing that any should perish, but that all should come to repentance, and surrender to Him. I also believe that the Bible is the infallible Word of God. 2000 of its prophecies have already come true, to the letter—what book or author can boast of that!

Steve Campbell

At age 16, I attended the annual church summer camp at Idlewild in the Southern California Mountains. My sophomore year in high school, 1962, I was pretty interested in girls, but very shy around them. While partaking of a small roundtable group discussion one afternoon, the counselor asked us "So what does Jesus mean to you?" I was sitting at the end of the circle, and as each of us was asked to share their knowledge of Jesus, something most incredible happened to me. I felt that what they were saying was what a counselor would expect to hear. As several of the group gave their answers, Jesus suddenly was at my right side, and at that moment I knew that what they were saying was true, but they hadn't experienced the reality of their words. Immediately, my heart became burdened for them to know that Jesus was REAL. Interestingly, I didn't know He was real either until that moment. The burden for the kids was spontaneous with the presence of Jesus. It was like He was in a body, though invisible to me. I was unable to bear the extreme reality of Jesus' presence and the accompanying feelings, so I had to leave the group, with a heavy heart and with tears streaming down my face. The camp week was nearing its end and there was to be a baptism for any who wanted to be baptized. I felt a very strong urge to be baptized, and I went to my counselor, who enquired whether or not I had already been baptized. I had, so he told me it was not necessary to be baptized again. I trustingly accepted his answer. From the moment I had experienced Jesus' presence beside me, I was no longer interested in girls, but only Jesus. So for the rest of the week I would go out into the woods alone and sing songs about Jesus, weeping and feeling the Spirit of God. I had been a Preacher's Kid for 25 years but had never heard the Gospel of salvation. I believe now that Jesus chose not to save me then, as I had not seen my need of a Savior. But I knew He was real!

I went back home that Saturday expecting that my father, the minister of a small Church in Fullerton, California, would be so happy that had I met Jesus. Well, I was sitting in the living room when he walked in and tears began to fall as I told him the wonderful news about my time at camp. Instead, he reacted in anger and said I could never go back to that camp, and he wanted to know who got my emotions all stirred up. And then he left the room. He later came back into the room and tried to explain that I had had a "mystical experience" as many sages from the past had. He explained that the Buddha had something similar, and so on. That was all new to me, but I figured he knew what he was talking about, being my father and a pastor. That next day was Sunday, and as I was taking communion, and a hymn about the cross was being sung, I couldn't hold back the tears. I didn't know about the Holy Spirit then, but He was moving on my heart then and for many more Sundays to come. No one recognized what was happening to me, and in time I lost those feelings that were so precious.

I never heard the Gospel in my 20 or so years growing up in the Church. It was not until I was twenty, while going home from a date in Whittier, California, when I stopped to get gas. There were gas attendants in those days; and while the attendant pumped gas, he asked me what I thought about Jesus. He proceeded to share the Gospel with me then, and for about seven years I would get letters from him, and then he sent Chick tracts in the mail. This wonderful soul winner never gave up on me for all those years. Just before I finally got saved he sent a Chick tract to my parents' house. I had never answered his letters or responded to him at all. Wow! When I finally heard the Gospel of salvation, I had become a slave to sin and was no longer interested. At 23, I moved to the California coast and began to study Eastern Religion and practice meditation.

My brother Craig and I were initiated the same day into Transcendental Meditation. That was Feb 14, 1972. Exactly one year later to the day, Craig and I were born again in a little cabin at Nepenthe. Several years before that I had a god experience while on LSD, after meditating on the *Bagavad Gita*. It was a powerful transcendental experience, a deceitful counterfeit of the Biblical "New Birth." The day a friend brought the book, *Be Here Now* by Baba Ram Das, I read it that night, and it was the exact experience I had just had that day. The next day on the beach, a stranger named Brendan Brooks came to the log I was sitting on and sat down by me. He began to tell me what I had experienced the day before. Needless to say, I was hooked. Brendan was moving to Big Sur a while later and asked me to join him and his little following. That was how I ended up in Big Sur. I never knew what Big Sur was until the night I arrived, seeing the lights of Nepenthe from the south just around the bend of Deetjen's Inn. As they say, this was a "magical place." Little does anyone know what God did there, and may yet do again.

I remember it as though it just happened. I had left Big Sur after an encounter with my landlord. He had quite upset the "guru" in me, and I felt for the first time in my life that I could kill someone. I was amazed at this revelation about myself, and well . . . was blown away to Orange County for several months in order to get my spiritual life together. I had previously had a psychotic break while on acid and was unsure just what was real. While visiting in my parents' home I read a book sitting on a table about juvenile crime and was very convicted of sin in my life. I could go to jail for the sins I had committed! I needed a teacher to guide me, as my self-guided discipline was no relief for the downward spiral my life was beginning to take.

I knew I could get a job back in Big Sur at Nepenthe, so I left Orange County after several months and returned to Big Sur. My plan was to make about 200 dollars and go to Kauai and study under a guru named Subramuniy. It was obvious I could not find the spiritual help I needed from books. I realized I needed a savior. I saw by now that I was lost spiritually, and was a sinner. Demonic powers were closing in on me, and they were very real.

So I arrived back in Big Sur around January 1973. While I had been away, several friends of mine became Jesus Freaks, and when they talked to me I could see they were very different. They had joy, and I had a sense of awe when around them (one of them was Brian Stanley). They talked to me in passing, telling me that Jesus was really in their lives and they were reading the Bible now. Their witness gave me the hope I desperately needed. I began to sing songs about Jesus for several days such as "Jesus Is Just All Right With Me", and "Put Your Hand in the Hand of the Man." As I sang these songs I began to sense light entering, and my soul was lifted up. Peace began to come to me, as I was now putting my hope in the Jesus of the Bible. That was the beginning of salvation. I realized then that I had been lost spiritually, felt conviction of my sin, and hoped then Jesus could help me.

While driving home from Monterey on February 14, 1973, I had asked my brother Craig to tell me what he had been learning while studying at an ashram in Europe as part of the Transcendental Meditation program. He shared some wisdom of the pundits, and I had to ask him to say it again, because it didn't even register in my brain. He restated what he had said, and at that point I saw that it was nonsense, and was in fact foolishness. Within a moment of that revelation, God spoke to me and said, "I want you to go to a Christian." I had never heard God speak and yet I knew beyond any doubt that it was in fact God Himself. I remember telling Craig that I couldn't understand anything he said, and for the rest of the drive to Nepenthe I said nothing. I was on my way to see if Annie Johnson was in her room. It was about 9:00 that evening and she was sitting up in her bed reading the Bible. She said to come in and I walked in, my heart bursting to tell her what had just happened and I fell on the end of the bed and wept as I said to her, "It's Jesus!" There, at that moment, I was saved. She said to me, "Isn't it wonderful to know the Lord?" She gave me a tape of songs recorded at a small meeting of Tom, Rita, Ruth, Mary, and Rachel and several others. I took the tape and sat down by a the fire in the plastic house cabin where Craig was lodging and played it, and wept at the wonderful revelations of Salvation, God's love, Calvary, Grace and the fact of a reality I had never thought existed, the body of Christ, the true brotherhood. It was a time of deep regret and remorse for my sin and true repentance. It was wonderful!

I got saved Feb 14, 1973, and was baptized on April 29 (Easter) somewhere along the Big Sur River with several of my brothers and sisters. It was the real thing, right out of the Bible. But the baptism of the Holy Ghost was a far more wonderful experience for me. Bro. Abbott was preaching that Sunday morning in the Rowe's home and there were Salinas Brethren and the Big Sur Brethren there.

The room was filled with brethren and the sweet power of the Holy Spirit was with us and there was seriousness in the air. At the end of the preaching the opportunity to be baptized in the Holy Spirit came about. Several were baptized. Days before this, some brethren had briefly spoken to me about tongues, saying that it would allow me to have more of God, and so now my opportunity had come. I got on my knees and the brethren gathered around and laid hands on me and they began to pray and sing in tongues. The room was filled with the most beautiful songs in the Spirit, made from harmonies of the saints and angels. It was holy! "Heaven came down and glory filled my soul."I didn't speak out with a powerful tongue, as I remembered others had done, but the Holy Spirit revealed to me, as I began to speak in tongues, that his Presence was inside me. He was revealed as the Ancient of Days, the Eternal One. It was not a mental picture, but an experience of the true God who dwelt so deeply within me. He was eternal, ancient, and holy. There was never a question concerning the speaking of tongues or the filling of the Spirit after that. It is true that God comes to live in us in a greater way after the Baptism of the Holy Ghost. I have since believed that all believers should have this wonderful baptism.

This was only the beginning of a lifelong relationship in which I have truly come to know the faithfulness, love, and beauty of the Living God.

Lois DeFord

There are many who would agree with me that the greatest meeting of land and sea on this earth happens in a place called Big Sur. I was very drawn to it when I was just out of high school in San Mateo, California. In 1968, when I was enrolled to attend San Francisco State University, student riots broke out there, and I decided to head south instead. I hitchhiked down to Big Sur, in answer to an invitation from a high school friend who was working at Deetjen's Big Sur Inn. I didn't know then she would be leaving soon for college, and I would take her place.

When I arrived, I fell in love, not only with the Inn, but also with Big Sur. I had never seen such a beautiful place, with majestic hills and mountains dropping down steeply into the undulating bluestof-blue seas that mirrored the azure sky. This vista, stretching as far as the eye could see, was both healing and transfixing. Huge stately redwoods in the cool canyons awed and inspired me. In response to such beauty, my soul could only leap for joy, and I felt I had come home.

My first job was cleaning rooms at Deetjen's Inn, and then I was offered the position of lunch cook. There I met Bob, my future husband, one December evening in 1968; we were introduced and shook hands in the kitchen. In June of 1969, we were married, up from the trail of Seven Dwarfs behind the Inn, in a place called The Enchanted Room, a small clearing by the stream ringed with ancient redwoods, and an old redwood stump served as an altar. Later, we had a beautiful baby boy, and Mary, the author of this book, attended his birth. We named our son Joshua Christian, a portent of things to come.

I loved my husband and my baby, but still felt emptiness within. The deep desire of my heart was to know the Truth. I continued my spiritual quest, seeking the Truth, but it remained elusive. Though my heart was grieved, I was mostly content and felt privileged to live in a very beautiful and spiritual place. My baby boy, the joy of my life, was growing up, and I had good friends. There was a lot for which to be thankful. However, when I looked to my future, I saw only dark clouds on my horizon, and sensed that the path I was on would not bring me to Truth and Life.

About two years later, in February of 1972, my friend Rita Gatti, who had a baby boy only two weeks before my son was born, had just had a life-changing experience and she was eager to tell me about it. Rita and I had shared many wonderful times with our little boys, and she was an incredible support to me. Paul Johnson, a musician friend of Tom Carvey, had come to Big Sur from a Christian commune up north in the Eureka area called The Lighthouse Ministry. He had shared the Gospel with them, and encouraged them to visit the commune and see for themselves. They did, and accepted Jesus, not really understanding what they had done. Life for them and for Big Sur would never be the same.

"Plant the good seeds of righteousness, and you will harvest a crop of love. Plow up the hard ground of your hearts, for now is the time to seek the LORD, that he may come and shower righteousness upon you." (Hosea 10:12)

Rita's life-changing event was she asked Jesus into her heart, and she shared with me how God was changing her life. I was intrigued, but still reluctant. It was very clear to me that I didn't want to join any hippie bandwagon or cult. My continuing prayer was that I would come to know the Truth, and not be sidetracked by any diversion, no matter how enticing. What I didn't fully realize then was, that despite my being raised in the American Baptist church, I was still under the bondage of sin and death, and what I was searching for was freedom from darkness. It wasn't that Jesus wasn't in the church, but I personally hadn't met Him there; perhaps because I looked too much to people, and not to Him.

One day, alone in my little cabin, after many heartfelt talks with Rita, I prayed that if Jesus were real, that He would clearly make Himself known to me, and not one doubt would remain in my mind. Without telephones or normal means of communication that very night, several Christians suddenly were gathered in my tiny living room, playing their guitars and singing songs about Jesus. My dear friends, Mary and Rita were there, and Tom and Sue Carvey, and perhaps one or two others I do not now recall.

I was simply amazed, and knew deep in my heart that God had answered my prayer. The next day, I prayed alone and asked Jesus to come into my heart. I was overwhelmed that the Truth for which I had so diligently searched had come to me! It took a few more days for me to realize that I was a sinner, lost in darkness, and then I repented with many tears before the Lord. After receiving His forgiveness, I felt so loved and cleansed for the first time in my life. Jesus showed me that He is "the Way, the Truth and the Life." By asking Him to come into my heart and yield my life to Him, I found the Truth for which I had so diligently searched. Knowing that Jesus is Truth personified is a deeply transformational experience because it sets us free. And at long last I had been set free. There was still much work to be done within me, as I had labored many years under false assumptions and an anxious mind. The first thing God gave back to me was hope, a real and tangible hope for my future.

Big Sur was the perfect place for me to find salvation, as its beauty lent itself to my spiritual awakening, and the Fellowship there became a very important part of my life for several years. The love I received from this wonderful group of people I have never experienced again. It was a time and place for God to do a special work, and I was privileged to be a part of it. I have remained so grateful to Rita, who never gave up on me, but continued to share her love and faith in a God she knew to be true, until I came to personally know Him and understand His ways. My husband had been at work, and missed the simple and yet profound gathering in our home that evening in February, but he did come to the Lord about two weeks later. God became the Father that he never had, and I was so grateful that we could journey on our new-found path together.

God has remained faithful to me, and kept me within His enfolding love as I continue to walk with Him, by His grace, down this path of life. He is with me every small step of the way. God has proven Himself so many times, answered my prayers, and protected me. The *transforming* power of His Love, Light, and Presence continues to guide me daily.

Lois DeFord
May 2012

Rita Gatti

I was furious with God (*I obviously believed there was a God, being raised in Catholicism*) because of the loss and cruelty I suffered as a child, and even for how He seemed to treat many of the martyrs . . . allowing them to die horrible deaths, etc. So I was not drawn to following God, serving God, or loving God, when He caught up with me during the move of God in the early 70s. I shook my fist at God . . . but I was so lost, and the responsibility of having brought a life into the world was so heavy on me, that there was a moment in time that I softened enough to ask God to prove Himself to me (*Cheeky girl that I was*). The response was immediate and it met the need of my heart in an instant. He spoke to my deepest need, not audibly of course, but I heard the words with my spirit and they were: "Everything has a purpose. I have a plan for the world." This answer completely disarmed my anger, and I had to rethink my worldview and address a lot of attitudes. I also needed to be re-educated in my relationships to authority and others. I still carry some attitudes that have shaped my life, but I have made peace with my past and all that has happened, including the Youth For Truth years, which for me were a mixture of agony and ecstasy. I find that I can be thankful instead of angry and to me that is fruit . . . whatever the cost. I am very thankful and feel very blessed that I can look at my past as part of what made me who I am, and I am not at war with whom I am.

My life has been and still is meaningful, and that seems to be very important to me. I can look at events in my own life and in the lives of others, community, country and the world with that view . . . so that while I am not a fatalist in any sense of the word, I do feel relatively comfortable with the mysteries being mysteries and the unknown being part of life, that some answers may never come forth in my lifetime, that things will not always go the way I would choose. I try not to be anxious about any thing—sometimes that is a challenge—but it comes easier as I get older. So in a nutshell: it is all part of the journey.

I feel the need to be careful about judging what God has done in my life. There is definitely fruit that I enjoy, so when I consider the path that I have come, I can just relegate it all to "God's mysterious ways."

James Laney

I grew up in a church-going home and did what was asked of me. I knew even then, however, that I was dead to the things of God. I had no interest; I didn't care. So when I went away to college, I was happy to leave religion far behind. But, between my junior and senior year, my father died suddenly and unexpectedly at the age of 48. I admired him greatly and was following in his footsteps, so my world was turned upside down.

Looking back, that was the beginning of a time of seeking that eventually led to a living faith in the living God some six years later. I looked for answers in political change, but I saw that the end result was only confrontation and hate. I then looked for answers in cultural change, exploring communal lifestyles, but saw that was a dead end for me. Finally I looked for answers in spiritual change, exploring a variety of Eastern religions; and, although I discovered nuggets of truth, after a time I saw these answers were not enough and I moved on, hungering for more.

I ended up in Big Sur, California, in 1972, and there encountered some folks who said they loved the Lord and seemed to me to be living their lives out in an authentic reflection of their faith. After some time observing them, I inquired about what their secret was. They told me Jesus was alive and I could know Him for myself. At a Wednesday night meeting, in a little cabin in Big Sur, they led me in prayer, and I asked Jesus to reveal Himself to me. They hooted and hollered, "Hallelujah, he's saved!" I didn't even know what I was and said to myself, "We'll see."

As I left they suggested I start reading the Gospel of John, and as I walked home that evening to my little cabin on the hill, considering all that had transpired, I looked up and saw the stars shining in a glory I had never seen before. I got back and opened up the Bible to the Gospel of John. By the time I got to the end of Chapter Four, God had revealed Himself to me and spoken to my heart and mind twice, quite clearly. First, that Jesus Christ was truly the only begotten Son of God, begotten, not made, of one being with the Father, God from God, Light from Light, words that I had repeated countless times in church growing up, but now for the first time were alive with meaning. Then, as I finished reading the story of the Samaritan woman at the well, the Lord said to me, "James, you have drunk of many earthly waters, haven't you?" And I said, "Yes, Lord, I have," thinking of the many, many streams I had drunk looking for purpose and meaning and fulfillment in my life. And He said, "Well, now I am going to give you living waters and you will thirst no more." And I said, "Do it, Lord," and opened my heart and mouth and mind.

For forty years now, seldom—no never—has a day gone by where I have not drunk from those waters. Some of those days have been dark and trying, some exhilarating, mountaintop experiences; some of the trials have been deep and long. But I have always, always known He is alive and with me; I have always enjoyed the living waters of the living God. He has always brought me through, and each time I have emerged a more mature Christian, more dependent on His grace, more aware of my poverty of spirit and His abundant mercy. The joy of knowing Him and always learning more carries me through day by day as I seek to serve Him in the work He has given me to do, learning more the way of the cross, stretched, again and again, learning to love, always, everywhere, everyone: absolute surrender, total trust, perfect love.

"The Lord is good;
His mercy is everlasting;
And His truth endures from generation to generation."

I should note that the author of this book, Mary Stewart, was instrumental in my coming to faith there in that cabin in Big Sur. One of the brothers had asked during their meeting, "What has the Lord done in your life this week, Mary?"And she said a few words that sounded hollow to me at first, but then, as she got a hold of what the Lord had been doing, it seemed genuine and real. Then she added, "Oh, and He gave me this song," which she proceeded to play. It melted my heart and I knew those folks had something that I wanted. A few minutes later, there I was on my knees, praying.

John Rowe

Raised in the Southern Baptist tradition, and having had a salvation experience with Jesus early on, I had come to know who Jesus was, but nevertheless fell to my own way.

Arriving in Big Sur some twenty-five years later with some Eastern religion studies under my belt, trying to attain total awareness, and thinking I had attained "all that," I was more than amazed by the power of the Holy Spirit, expressed through a believer during a meeting. Later on, the baptism of the Holy Spirit touched the uttermost core of my being, and for the first time awakened me to discover who Jesus Christ really IS. It was as clear as the invisible atmosphere around us . . . that REAL! To be reborn by the Holy Spirit is as real as gravity.

Bro. Abbott was a man *on fire* for the Lord. There were many times in the early days of our Fellowship when he would speak forth the Word of God, or expound on its truths, that I would hear (with my spiritual ears) echoing claps of thunder, as if to underscore the Truth of God's reality with a resounding, gigantic YES! And I knew then, as I now still know, that my life would never be the same.

Carol Smith

I came to Big Sur as a young, single mother searching for God, having heard there was a group of Christians there that knew and followed the Lord. I lived first in the campground at Ventana Inn and immediately got a job at Nepenthe, where I met a number of young Christians who worked there, including Steve Campbell and his younger brother Craig, Lois DeFord, Kim and John Rowe, and James Laney. Ruth was still working there as a chef, and Mary cooked in the Family Kitchen. I tried to join their Bible study around the kitchen table as they shared scriptures the Lord had given them, but since I wasn't saved then, they did not include me. There may have been some persecution toward the group then by some of the unsaved.

The first person I was introduced to in Big Sur was Arlene Carvey, who was a great help to me both with practical needs and as a witness for Christ. I was saved in the mid-week meeting at the DeFord's home. It was the third Tuesday in July 1973, and I had been in Big Sur only six weeks. I do remember Annie, later Annie Campbell, asking me why I didn't just ask the Lord into my heart and get saved, sensing that that was what I wanted. Hands were laid on me and everyone prayed. That night I heard angels glorifying God blended together with the prayers and praise of the brethren, and I remembered the scripture from Luke 15:10 that I had known from my childhood: "there is rejoicing in the presence of God over one sinner who repents." I also had a place in that little complex for a while and Barbara Rightmeyer was my next-door neighbor.

Shortly after my salvation experience, two things happened: I moved to the tool shed on Pfeiffer Ridge, and I worked for Crile Carvey in the deli at Ventana. Eileen was already the manager of the health food store at Ventana and we became friends there. I also cleaned houses for the waitress at Ventana whose husband had sculpted Nepenthe's *Dark Angel*. Later I moved down the hill and rented the worst trailer in the world. I was working in Monterey for a dentist, and while I was at work, Ruth and someone whose name I don't remember cleaned that pit from front to back and made it livable. That was a real testimony to the love of the brethren there. There were many other incidents but that one deeply touched me, and I have never forgotten the love they had shown me.

Life in Big Sur for me was a real healing and rest for my soul. To get up in the morning and go outside and see the fog on the ocean, breathe clean air, and know that I belonged to the Lord of the universe was such a rest from the world and a balm for my soul. I also loved the outdoor shower. We used to go to town about once a week and do our shopping and laundry in Carmel. One day I ran into Barbara and Marsha there. They wanted to go to lunch and asked to borrow money. I gave them all the money I had ($6) and went home broke that day. But when I got home, there was a letter for me from someone I never expected to hear from in Seattle. They too had borrowed some money from me, and I never thought I'd see it and had forgotten all about it. There was $10 in the letter. I saw the hand of God in the timing.

The Lord would give Steve Campbell music to put scripture to song and he would sing these songs and play his guitar in our little mid-week meetings at the Grange Hall. Those beautiful songs were so anointed.

There were lots of funny things that happened too. Like the time Annie was run out of her VW bus by a raccoon near Crile and Arlene's trailer at Ventana. It wasn't funny to her at the time, but it has made for a good story for us all ever since.

Epilogue

Book Two (*Journey into Liberty*) will cover the years 1976–2007, in which the author meets her future husband, John Anthony, a Marine Viet-Nam combat veteran; their miracle marriage in 1980; their years of discipleship in Winham St. Chapel; their subsequent release to the mission fields of Central and South America; and finally to China, the land of their calling. They continue to serve as Missionary Associates with the Assemblies of God, both at home and abroad.

CPSIA information can be obtained at www.ICGtesting.com
Printed in the USA
LVOW131217160613

338769LV00003B/517/P